VEGETABLE, FRUIT
GROWING IN SMALL SPACES

ABOUT THE AUTHOR

John Harrison, who has been described as 'Britain's greatest allotment authority' (*Independent on Sunday*), lives in the north-west of England with his wife Val. The shortage of available space in their garden led to their growing fruit and vegetables in containers on their small concrete patio. Although now their two allotments provide much of the food they eat, they still grow herbs and salad crops in pots at home. They also enjoy their own homemade bread, butter, jams and chutneys, as well as home reared eggs, and often drink their own beer and wine.

John runs two popular websites: **www.allotment.org.uk** and **www.lowcostliving.co.uk**. He is the author of four other books in the *Right Way* series:

Vegetable Growing Month by Month
The Essential Allotment Guide
Low-Cost Living – Live better, spend less

and, together with wife Val, **Easy Jams, Chutneys and Preserves**.

VEGETABLE, FRUIT AND HERB GROWING IN SMALL SPACES

John Harrison

RIGHT WAY

Constable & Robinson Ltd
3 The Lanchesters
162 Fulham Palace Road
London W6 9ER
www.constablerobinson.com

First published by Right Way, an imprint of
Constable & Robinson, 2010

A copy of the British Library Cataloguing in Publication Data
is available from the British Library

ISBN: 978-0-7160-2245-9

Printed and bound in the EU

1 3 5 7 9 10 8 6 4 2

CONTENTS

AT-A-GLANCE GUIDE

What you can grow on a window sill indoors
Basil
Chervil
Chives
Lettuce
Lemon grass
Marjoram
Mint
Parsley
Salad leaves
Spring onions
Thyme

What you can grow in a hanging basket or window box
Beetroot
Cranberries
Lettuce and Salad leaves
Lingonberries
Oregano
Parsley
Radish
Strawberries
Tumbler tomatoes
Turnips

What you can grow on a balcony/patio in pots	
Apples	Leeks
Bay leaves	Lemons
Beetroot	Limes
Blackcurrants	Mint
Blueberries	Oregano
Cabbage	Parsnips
Carrots	Pears
Cauliflowers	Peas
Cherries	Peppers
Coriander	Plums
Courgettes	Potatoes
Cucumbers	Redcurrants
Damsons	Rosemary
Dill	Runner beans
Figs	Sage
French beans	Salsify
French climbing beans	Scorzonera
Gages	Strawberries
Goji berries	Tarragon
Gooseberries	Tomatoes
Grapes	Turnips

INTRODUCTION

Over the 30 years I've been growing our own fruit and vegetables we've not always been fortunate enough to have a large garden to grow in. As a general rule, the more modern the house, the smaller the garden seems to be. Our first house, being a standard pre-war semi, had a 100' x 30' back garden but, as the years have moved on, builders have crammed more and more houses per acre so that now a house valued at a king's ransom has a garden space no bigger than many of the back to back terraced houses of yesteryear.

Currently we have a postage stamp garden but I'm fortunate to have an allotment around the corner to grow in but, with an estimated 100,000 people on waiting lists for a plot nationally, that's ceasing to become an option for most of us. Still, if you seriously want to grow your own, it's worthwhile checking what is available in your area.

The house we lived in before had a reasonable garden on a slope but the previous owner had made it into a series of concrete patios and terraces. There was one small soil border but otherwise just a lot of concrete. It was actually more attractive than it sounds with dwarf walls and pastel painting, but hardly a gardener's garden.

This set me a challenge to say the least. The prospect of hiring road digging jack-hammers to dig it up and skips to cart away the resulting rubble was hardly appealing. Not only would it have been a lot of work but financially costly as well.

Having thought about it, I realized that the only answer was to grow in containers. After all, the show growers with their superb specimens of perfect vegetables at shows like Chelsea and Tatton Park rarely stoop to planting in soil. Most of their growing is done under cover in containers so I knew it was possible. If you can grow flowers in a pot, why not vegetables?

Now I'm not into token growing. We like to eat as much of our own produce as possible. There are few things more satisfying than sitting down to a meal where most if not all of the food on the plate has been grown and raised yourself.

I'm not a strictly organic grower by any means but that doesn't mean I want to eat food loaded with pesticide residues that cannot be tasted, in fact that can only be detected by sophisticated chemical analysis. The government may assure us they are safe but nobody really knows if the combination of chemicals does us any harm.

It's fairly easy to find out what a safe level is for any particular chemical. Crudely, feed some to laboratory rats and see how much it takes to kill them. But if we have a little of this chemical, a smidgeon of that chemical and then throw yet another into the mix, nobody does know how dangerous the food we eat is in the long term. This is generally referred to as 'the cocktail effect'. With hundreds of different chemicals, the combinations run into the astronomical.

By growing your own you are in control. You know exactly what, if any, chemicals have gone into producing your food. Unlike the farmer, you can afford the time to use organic methods. There is no way around it, generally organic growing takes more labour than chemical growing. When you see organic produce in the supermarket, the question isn't why it is expensive; the question is how do they manage to do it for the price they do!

I believe growing your own, even just a small portion of what you eat, is important. It's a move towards self-sufficiency and freedom from a system that would reduce us to mere consumers. It creates a relationship between us and the seasons, reconnecting us with the world in a more concrete way than just deciding if we need to wear a sweater or carry an umbrella.

By growing your own you appreciate the value of food. So what if this carrot is a strange shape or that lettuce has been nibbled by a pest? I always say if it isn't good enough for a bug then it's not good enough for me!

There are many reasons for growing your own, even if only enough to make a small contribution to your needs but, selfishly, the most important to me is taste. You cannot beat home grown for freshness unless you have a 'pick your own' farm next door. The flavour of something you've grown yourself is always better.

Of all the vegetables we grow, the crop that shows the most benefit in flavour is the humble potato. It's hard to believe that our potatoes are the same species as those bought from the shops.

Home grown vegetables can save you money, although to be honest not if you include your labour and definitely not if you succumb to every gadget and gizmo advertised in the gardening magazines and on show at the garden centre. Still, by being inventive and recycling, you can save some money. There are not many hobbies that can actually make you a profit.

The last, but not least, reason for home growing is the planet we all share. We've all heard about air miles, beans being imported from Kenya and strawberries flown in from Israel. Even crops grown in the UK still end up being trucked up and down the motorway, creating a significant carbon footprint in the process.

Home grown uses next to nothing in comparison. A packet of seeds in the post produces a whole field of cabbages! At the same time, it puts you in touch with the seasons and the natural world. You're not going to stop climate change by yourself, but if we all do a little, then the total effect is massive.

If you have children, showing them where the food comes from and how it has to be nurtured to get there, is a far more effective teaching tool than muttering about people starving in far off lands and giving in to demands for processed rubbish.

Who is this book for?

Quite simply, this book is for anyone who wants to provide as much of his or her own produce as is possible from a small space. This could be as little as a balcony or even a fire escape which a friend of ours used until she was told she was creating a hazard.

Even if you have a reasonably sized garden, not all of it may be available to grow produce in. After all, gardens are multi-purpose areas. They feed the soul with beauty as well as providing a playing field for children, not to mention the two days a year when the weather lets us have a barbecue.

I mentioned my allotment above but a lot of people just don't have the time to allocate to looking after a large area of land. If you have just a few square metres or half a dozen pots to look after, then a few minutes a day is all you need.

Having had jobs that were demanding to say the least, I know the last thing you want to do when you finally get some free time is cope with a huge out of control plot with weeds so high you suspect a tribe of pygmies is hiding in there.

Incidentally, if you do work away from home a lot, then you can automate watering quite cheaply so your plants are looked after until you are around again.

What I hope to pass on through this book is the result of my researches and our experience growing our own from containers in a concrete garden. I hope to show you how to get the maximum production from what little space and time you have available.

You'll find that small space growing is actually more productive than you might think possible if you follow a basic plan. For the purposes of this book I'm going to assume you either have a small modern garden doing double duty as play area as well as vegetable plot or no garden at all, just some patio or balcony space.

If you have a larger area to work with or an allotment, then I'd suggest that my *Vegetable Growing Month by Month* and/ or *Essential Allotment Guide* would also be of value for you.

Having said that, despite having the allotments, we grow our herbs and most of our salad crops at home. It's far more convenient to nip out the back for a sprig of rosemary or a few spring onions than trek around to the allotment. Our minarette fruit trees will come with us in their pots on moving day unlike an apple tree on the plot. So even if you have the space, it can be useful to know small space and pot growing techniques.

I'd like to acknowledge the help I've had in writing this book from various members of the National Vegetable Society. The society organizes vegetable shows and competitions and many of the members are show growers who try not so much for giant vegetables as for perfect specimens. Most often they grow these vegetables in containers and pots and they have happily passed on many tips to me.

Unfortunately, if you ask two gardeners for an opinion or method you are likely to get at least three answers. I've given my tried and tested methods for getting good results, but you may well find that other methods work just as well or even better for you in your circumstances.

I've covered what I feel to be the best compost mixes and methods but don't be a slave to the technicalities. Home growing is an art more than a science. Work with what you have and don't be afraid to adapt and alter. More often than not you will still succeed and whatever happens you will learn. Home growing should be a pleasure, not a chore.

Finally, above all, I'm practical in my approach. In theory you can grow anything in a container, but I see little point in trying to grow those plants that would need an impracticably large pot or take up a disproportionate amount of room in a small garden. I've listed some crops that I think you really should give a miss in a small garden with the reason why not to grow them and hopefully you will agree.

1

WHAT TO GROW IN AND WHERE

Like most things in life, success with small space and container growing involves some planning, some work and some luck. Luck is critical to all gardening, if by luck you mean the weather. We can add water, we can add nutrients, we can fight off the pests but adding sunshine is beyond most of us.

You may have noticed that weeds will pop up anywhere: in the shade under a tree, cracks in a pavement, even a hole in a wall. Sadly the crops we eat aren't quite so tough. Over the years we've bred our crops for our needs, not theirs, and so they're a lot fussier than the weeds.

They need sunlight if they're to thrive. The more sunlight, the more energy is available for the plant's solar power plant to convert into leaf and fruit, so the sunnier the better.

Now you may think you have light enough but the human eye is a marvellous instrument. In bright sunlight our pupils contract and in low light they expand so we can see in quite a range. In fact we're hardly aware of the difference; walk around the corner into shade and our eyes adapt without our needing to do anything. Any photographer will tell you that light levels vary tremendously, whatever our eyes tell us.

Basically if you're facing south, then your plants will have plenty of direct sunlight. To the east they'll get full sun in the morning and to the west in the afternoon but facing to the north they're going to struggle. It's not impossible to grow in north-facing places but avoid if you can. Similarly avoid shade if you can as well.

There is an exception to this rule, of course. You can grow a morello cherry trained up a north-facing wall.

The trick to getting the most from small spaces is to think and plan in four dimensions. Now don't worry, we're not moving into Dr Who territory with four dimensions, but time and planning ahead are critical to success.

The first two dimensions, length and breadth, give us the area we have to grow in. Because we're going to be providing the ideal nutrition for our plants we can grow more densely than normal and gain yields nearly double that of conventional planting. Large area growing usually has vegetables in orderly rows with a spacing that allows for hoeing off weeds. Because we crowd our plants, the weeds get little chance to grow and those that do dare to pop their head up are soon pulled out by hand. Weeding a pot or small bed is the work of a minute.

Since we're working with a small area we can give far more attention per plant than on a large plot. This means we pick up developing problems early and get them sorted. For example, some butterfly eggs can go unnoticed when you have a dozen cabbages but you are going to spot them before they turn into ravenous caterpillars and eat half the plant when you have just two or three plants growing.

The third dimension is, of course, height. Some plants provide huge value for the area they use. Tomatoes growing up a stake are incredibly productive, producing pounds of fruit from half a square foot area. Fruit trees trained up a wall will provide all you can eat from next to no square footage.

Hanging baskets aren't just for flowers, tumbler tomatoes can look just as attractive as surfinias, and strawberries can be grown in hanging baskets too. You can get flower pouches which are hung on a wall and use these for strawberries as well.

A strawberry barrel with fruit planted into the side will provide enough strawberries for the family and some pots of jam for the cupboard in very little space. Compared with conventional planting you get about eight times as many plants per square foot using a barrel planter. This is just a barrel shaped tub, often called a strawberry tower, with holes let into the sides into which the plants are set.

You won't believe how many potatoes you can get from growing in a bag or barrel. Incidentally, the top show growers always grow their potatoes in bags of special compost rather than the soil used by mere mortals.

Growers with space to spare may bother to do something called underplanting but it's doubtful. They think in terms of rotation plans and this goes here and that goes there. Small space growers do not want to see any bare soil so there is always something that can go under the tomatoes or in that space where the cabbage was. Lettuce often benefit from some shade in hot summers so they're good for planting in the shady spots. Got a square inch spare? Pop a couple of radishes or spring onions in.

The fourth dimension is time. Having made the most of not every square inch but every cubic inch of space we now need to think of timing. A full grown lettuce with a spread of, say, 6 inches needs 113 square inches. Yet at the start of its life it only needs a tiny bit of space.

By using our precious space most efficiently, growing in small pots and modules before planting out in the final position, we can effectively treble our growing area. This concept of successional sowing and planting is the key to maximum production from the smallest spaces.

I start my tomatoes off by sowing in a 3 inch (8cm) shallow pot, which can easily give me a dozen plants. Once they've grown a little they move into a 3 inch pot each. By the way, you can buy square pots which means you don't waste the space between circular pots. The plants may even go up a pot before ending up in their final planting spot or pot. This may all sound very utilitarian and regimented but gardens and patios should be attractive to the eye as well as the stomach. Interplanting with flowers will add to the visual appeal and can help your crop yield by distracting pests. There is actually a variety of trailing marigold sold especially to tomato growers to ward whitefly away.

We like to grow a dwarf bush tomato in a jardinière with trailing lobelia below. They look decorative and with just two plants, we cover our salad tomatoes for the season. See Fig. 1.

Fig. 1. Tomatoes in a jardinière with trailing flowers.

The runner bean was grown for many years not for its beans but as a decorative plant. Indeed, the beans were thought poisonous! Painted Lady is considered the prettiest runner bean and the beans are very good to eat as well.

A strawberry can be interplanted with decorative trailers in a hanging basket to provide a bonus crop.

Although you can, in theory, grow anything in a container, some crops are more suitable than others and give better yields for the space they use. Of those that do make sense to grow in a small space, choosing the right varieties will make your small space even more productive. I've covered this in the individual fruit and vegetable listings.

The Small Garden

If we look at the average modern estate garden with limited space, then fitting in some crops may seem difficult. A goodly portion will be taken up with a patio area to start with. I wouldn't suggest getting rid of the patio; after all, we need somewhere to hold the annual barbecue on the summer's day when it doesn't rain.

But patios usually have more space than we need for a barbecue and table set, so this gives us an opportunity to grow some crops in pots.

Back into the garden area itself, there's usually a lawn. Now apart from being the traditional centre piece for the borders, lawns provide a playing field for the children. From games of cricket to just somewhere to run off some energy, a place to pitch the tent and to have an exciting picnic, the lawn is fairly vital and well used so, here again, I'd hesitate to suggest you got rid of it. However, you might be able to get away with pinching some space for crops from it.

If you don't have children using the lawn, do you really want it? The weekly ritual of mowing in the season and digging out the dandelions takes more time than growing most crops would. In that situation I'd consider getting rid of the lawn and replacing it with paths and raised beds.

The borders provide the last element of a garden. They are attractive to the eyes and nose. Now the French are undoubtedly the masters of the potager garden. They've been growing in potagers for 400 years and the name itself comes from the vegetables grown for the soup or 'potage'. This is an ornamental garden where, instead of flowers, they grow vegetables or a mix of flowers and vegetables. I'd contend that a red cabbage or red frilly leaved lettuce like lollo rosso is as dramatic and decorative as any foliage plant you can get, except the rainbow chard – and you can eat the chard.

Carrots with their fern-like, feather foliage can add definition while curly kale acts as a taller structural element in the design.

Often the potager is designed in a very formal manner, squares and triangles abound or even a similar style to a knot garden. Potagers are a wonderful way to balance the decorative and productive elements of a small garden. The gardens of the palace at Versailles in France had to provide for the royal table without offending their majesties' eyes. So the

Fig. 2. Making the most of the space available.

largest example of the potager was created for them covering 21 acres!

A multitude of small beds takes a lot of looking after though so consider just planting in larger beds but using those design elements. Treat your vegetables in the same way you might treat bedding plants.

You can define the edge of a path using a stepover apple or, instead of the traditional edging box, rosemary. For taller structural pieces why not try a red variety of Brussels sprout like Falstaff or the Petit Posy, which is a cross breed of kale and sprout producing 'rosettes' of loose frilly edged buttons on a long stalk, in purples, greens and bicoloured leaves?

A tepee with climbing beans can really add visually to the centre of a bed. Try the purple podded French or the good old English runner as mentioned above. A bay leaf in a pot can do the same job, being moved to a more sheltered area when the cold weather arrives.

The fence around the garden provides a support to run climbing plants up or, better still, to train a range of fruit trees up. The range of styles you can train trees into means you can fit them into your garden's style: a fan trained tree for less formal gardens or straight sided for more formal styles. Once your imagination gets going, the sky's the limit.

The cottage garden is the English version of the French potager. Here we're less formal and the emphasis, nowadays at least, is more on the flowers but there's no reason not to go back to its origins and mix in the crops with the flowers.

The Front Garden

So who decreed that the front garden was exempt from being useful? Everything I've suggested for the back garden can be done at the front. OK, the neighbours might be a bit curious and think you a little mad at first but who's the mad one? The person tending a bit of lawn by the car parked in the drive or the person harvesting a crop from that space?

Raised Beds

Raised beds are becoming popular even where people have lots of space to grow in but their real value comes in where space is tight. Effectively you can double the yield by growing in a raised bed and they define a separate area that you can hopefully stop the children from charging through.

The ideal size for a raised bed is 10' x 4' (3m x 1.2m). This allows you to easily reach into the centre of the bed from either side and isn't so long that you are tempted to hop across the bed rather than walk around. Don't forget you need paths wide enough to get round easily with a wheelbarrow.

You don't have to have 10' x 4' beds – you might just have a metre square or even a circular bed. I don't really like triangular beds though – too much space is wasted in the corners.

The edging of the bed can be made from various materials. The cheapest is wood which also looks very attractive. Ideally you want a wood that won't rot despite being in contact with the ground so treating with a preservative is a must. Cuprinol is very good when used in accordance with the instructions but other makes can be bought. Check that the preservative is suitable for wood in contact with the soil (fence stain won't do the job). You can also get different shades and colours if you want to be fashionable.

Try contacting scaffolding contractors as they often have secondhand boards going for a song. Scaffold boards are ideal being around 8 inches (20cm) deep and an inch (2.5cm) thick. Using pressure injected fence posts to make a corner and some pressure treated 2" x 1" (5cm x 2.5cm) for external braces you can easily construct your own in a few hours.

If you have the corner posts slightly raised, they can be useful to stop hosepipes dragging over the beds and, with the addition of the finial balls similar to those used for staircases, look very decorative.

An easier but more expensive way with wooden beds is to buy them in kit form. Harrod Horticultural offer a wide range of different beds in kit forms at surprisingly reasonable prices, including beds designed to fit into a corner. You can also get cloche and netting kits specifically designed to fit on top of the beds.

Plastic raised bed kits are another option. The best I've found on the market are Link-a-bord™. These come in a modular component form so you can construct different sizes and depths of bed along with add-on kits to provide cloches and net butterfly protection, etc., as with the wooden kits above.

The reason I really like Link-a-bord, as incidentally do a lot of the show growers, is the boards are two sided which means they are less likely to warp and bend under the pressure of the soil. The gap in the middle provides an insulating air-gap as well, helping the soil to keep warm at the end of the season.

There's nothing to stop you constructing brick sides to raised beds, particularly if you want an unusual shape like a curved bed. Do ensure the bricks are well grouted on both sides to avoid providing a home for pests.

We once constructed a raised bed edged with natural stone like the stone walls found edging country lanes. Unfortunately, this was a disaster. It held the soil and looked very attractive but it also provided housing for millions of slugs and snails. A lesson learned.

Another unusual edging I've seen used was wine bottles placed neck-end down. Not immensely practical but attractive none the less. Of course it's quite a job drinking all the wine, but it can be done.

Because the beds are raised, once built they're easier for those of us with bad backs, etc. You can get a handy kneeler stool so you can sit or kneel next to the bed and use the handles to get back up.

Incidentally, with all raised beds, one important principle is that you never tread on the beds. The reason is that treading will compact the soil structure and so you'll need to dig over to get air into the soil and maintain the structure. Much easier just not to tread on it and rely instead on the cultivation of your crops to keep the soil light.

Building A Raised Bed
However you edge your bed, the construction method is basically the same. Mark out the area using peg and line and check it's square. To check a corner is square we use Pythagoras's theorem

known to joiners the world over as a 3, 4, 5 square. From the corner mark a point 3 units – feet or metres doesn't matter as long as you use the same throughout. On the other straight edge mark a point 4 units from the corner. The diagonal that connects them should be 5 units if the corner is a right angle.

If you're converting a portion of lawn into a raised bed, remove the turves about 2 inches (5 cm) deep and place to one side. Next take up any good top soil and place that to one side – in a barrow or on a tarpaulin is idea.

Next dig over the underlying soil. If it is clay, then add some bags of pea gravel and sharp sand. Clay is made of very small particles, and sand particles are larger so the sand will break up the clay and further help drainage.

Now fix your edging in place and place the turf removed earlier grass side down and chop up a little with the spade, adding the top soil over that and then adding whatever compost you have to hand, building up to an inch or two (2.5–5cm) below the edging. Exhausted compost from old pots and tubs can be used for this.

Leave the bed for as long as you can to settle; a month is good or the whole winter if you have it. Under the soil the worms will be moving in, breaking up those turves, mixing the sub-soil with the top soil and creating drainage holes. Wonderful creatures, worms.

You now have a very productive growing area. The depth of the good quality soil is what allows you to plant so closely.

Very Deep Beds for Reduced Mobility
If you have a real problem with getting down to ground level, then you can build waist-height raised beds. These are also useful for enabling the wheelchair user to continue gardening. Obviously it's critical to make sure the paths to and surrounding the beds are wide enough for the wheelchair.

Check how far the wheelchair user can reach in comfortably and construct the bed just under twice that width so they'll be able to easily reach the middle from either side. It can be a strain working to the side so we don't want to make it worse by continual stretching to the centre.

Fig. 3. Very deep bed with wheelchair user.

For those who aren't in a chair but have mobility problems and use a frame or sticks, then consider fixing grab rails to the sides of the beds.

Now the big problem with beds at waist height is the pressure of soil causing the sides to bulge and warp, especially when wet. You can use brick, but here you need either to be a good brick-layer or to get one in. In effect you're building retaining walls and a good bricklayer will know how to do this.

There is, however, a simple and economical way to build very deep beds. Buy the concrete fence posts that have a groove to set the panels in and fix these firmly into concrete about 12 inches (30cm) deep so they will not move. There will be more pressure on the posts than with a fence so it's important they are rock solid. This should leave enough post standing to slot your boards into. Then slot in two of the concrete gravel boards designed to go under the fence panels, one above the other. Some suppliers will provide the gravel boards at special sizes or cut them down for you on request so you can build your bed to your requirements.

These concrete beds can look very clinical and unattractive. However, you can hide them behind willow hurdles or paint the concrete with milk or milk with plain yogurt mixed in to encourage the growth of lichens and age the concrete. Once the new edge is off they look a lot better.

If you just fill your deep beds with soil or compost, then drainage will become a problem. Over time the material will compact and can become waterlogged and sour. There is little point in filling it anyway as most vegetables will be fine in 18 inches (45cm) or less of compost. There are a few exceptions, such as long carrots and parsnips, but as a rule 18 inches is all you need.

Fill the first 18 inches with a mixture of rubble and gravel, breaking up the soil below if it's a hard clay pan first. This will ensure easy draining. Top up above with your compost and you're ready to go.

Trestle Bed
The 'fault' with waist-high beds for wheelchair users is that they're forced to work to the side. If we can construct a bed like a table where the chair can go under, then it's possible to work face on.

Now the problems here are two fold, depth and weight. If the bed is too deep, then it will be really awkward to use but, luckily, many vegetable crops will be perfectly happy in just 6 inches (15cm) of compost so long as there are plenty of nutrients present.

Don't under-estimate the weight of the soil. Incidentally, this applies to the waist-high beds and any container growing. The exact weight will depend on the moisture content and composition of the soil/compost mixture. A bed 6 inches (15cm) deep, 6 feet x 3 feet (2m x 1m) will contain 10.5 cubic feet (0.3 cubic metres) which is the same as four 75 litre bags of multi-purpose compost. If there is sand in the mix, which is a higher density than compost, the weight will be much greater and then we have the water content to consider. The water fills the gaps between the particles so we could be looking at around 176 pints (100 litres) or more of water in the same space. One litre of water weighs 1kg (at 20°C to be exact) so the total weight of our trestle bed could be 57 stone (360kg).

You can see from this that a table style bed needs to be carefully constructed with firm supports. Don't forget drainage holes in the base either. If, like pots, you cover the holes with some broken clay pot shards it will stop the holes blocking with compost.

Container Growing

If you've not got the room for raised beds or, as we found ourselves, with a garden covered in concrete, then it has to be container growing. Now even though I currently have two allotments to grow in, I use containers for much of our salad crops and for carrots and parsnips.

The easy way to obtain containers is to just go and buy them from the garden centre. You can get a huge range of shapes and sizes in everything from plastic to wood, metal to glazed finishes.

Being of the mind that there is little point in growing your own if you have to spend a fortune to do it, I've a few tips that will save you money. If you are buying from the shops, try to pick the end of the season when there will be bargains to be had. With pottery, check over for small chips and marks. Point them out to the staff and ask for an extra discount. One chap just threw a pot in for us that had started the season at £33! We had bought quite a bit already but it goes to show it is worth asking.

With pottery, always tap the pot. If there is a crack in it, the ring will be dull, quite distinct from the bell like tone of a perfect pot.

When buying terracotta pots, check they are frostproof. Many foreign imports from warmer climes will crack when the winter comes.

You can decorate your own pots. The plain terracotta type can be transformed by painting the rim and using a stencil or freehand if you are artistic to put a design on. We just used ordinary exterior gloss paint we had left over from decorating.

It's always worth keeping an eye out at car boot sales or even when passing skips. We picked up a 1 metre tub for just £3 like that.

In the supermarkets where they sell cut flowers, they often sell off the pots they come in for pennies – eight for a pound being common. You'll need to drill some drainage holes in the base but they're a tenth of the price of buying plastic pots and just as good.

Don't forget that when you're putting pots together in a group on the patio, the ones at the back won't be visible. So you can use attractive pots at the front and cheap pots at the back.

Since there's nothing to stop you mixing flowers and productive crops, using trailing plants like lobelia you won't see the pot and can get away with plain pots even where appearance is important.

Plastic pots are generally a lot cheaper but I prefer them as a rule since they're easier to clean, are frostproof and retain water better. Unglazed pottery pots allow water to evaporate through the sides so dry out much more quickly in warm weather.

When you're starting plants off you'll find you need a lot of small pots. You can use those disposable cups that dispense drinks from vending machines. Our local garage has one of these in the waiting room and the owners were happy to donate the used cups. A quick swill in water and we had more small pots than we needed.

There are a multitude of household items that convert into unusual growing containers. Old Belfast style sinks used to be easy to find but since they became fashionable, they're difficult to get – at a reasonable price anyway. On a pottery theme, the most unusual container I've seen is an old toilet pan.

Cheap plastic buckets can often be cheaper than plastic pots of similar size to buy, although I cannot believe they're cheaper to make. For a really big pot, you can source used barrels. Check what they were used for though. Foodstuffs are fine but if they contained chemicals, check for safety. I saw a pile at a factory and asked but they told me they had contained a chemical and were hazardous waste. Anyway, if you get a plastic barrel, cut in half to make two large tubs or lengthways to make two long troughs. The important thing is to use your imagination with containers.

With pots and containers, don't forget you need good drainage. If water builds up in the bottom of the pot, then the plant may well drown. If you just put compost into a larger pot, then it may well compact and block the drainage holes so cover these drainage holes with bits of broken pot or even pieces of polystyrene so the water can get out.

Specialist Containers

I've often seen clay strawberry pots for sale that are just too small. If you're going to grow strawberries you need a reasonable size container or the compost dries out really quickly and you'll have poor plants at best.

I found a Victorian style strawberry tower holding 80 litres of compost and 32 plants brilliant. It's quite attractive despite

Fig. 4. Strawberry barrel.

being plastic and when the strawberries fruit it looks beautiful. It only takes up a few square feet yet keeps us in fresh strawberries through the summer with enough over to provide some delicious jam as well.

You can buy a potato barrel in a similar style to the strawberry tower but if you're not so bothered about looks there's a range of large growing bags and sacks on the market or you can even use an old compost bag with some drainage holes poked into it. The show growers always grow in bags about the size of a two gallon bucket (one seed potato per bag).

Another method for potatoes and to provide large tubs is to use old tyres as bottomless containers. While I'm all in favour of recycling, I'm not so keen on acquiring something that requires specialist disposal if I change my mind.

For growing tomatoes, you can buy an upside down container. This is rather like a tubular hanging basket and the tomato grows downwards. They're said to promote heavier crops and earlier ripening but my experience was that the plant curled upwards, was difficult to keep pruned and neither

Fig. 5. Upside down tomato pot.

ripened earlier nor cropped heavier. However, some people have told me they're wonderful so perhaps it was just bad luck on my part.

One excellent new product on the market is the Patiogro system, invented by Peter Wolfenden. This is a patio growing system based around a metal frame forming three shelves into which extra deep planting trays are sat. The extra depth makes them ideal for a range of crops from salads and herbs to carrots and strawberries. A cover can be placed over the whole frame, turning it into a greenhouse and there is even a micro irrigation system available.

Grow Bags

The grow bag has a lot to answer for. They've convinced more people that tomatoes are hard to grow than anything else you can think of. The initial concept was excellent. A long bag in which you can grow, holding in the moisture and avoiding any weed problems. At the end of the year, the exhausted compost would provide a soil conditioner.

Fig. 6. Patiogro set up.

The fact is that competition drives price down and so grow bags have shrunk in size and the quality of the compost inside has become awful in many cases. So the first rule with grow bags is not to go for the cheapest in the DIY shed. You pays your money and takes your choice!

I've seen grow bags used by cutting into two and up-ending them to make two large plastic bag pots. Personally I'd rather use two large pots but it is a quick solution if you haven't any large pots.

For growing salad crops, a decent grow bag is perfectly adequate but for tomatoes, peppers and aubergines they have two problems. First, they just don't contain enough compost for the best results in my opinion. Tomatoes are particularly vulnerable to drying out which can cause split skins and blossom end rot so having a larger amount of compost to act as a reservoir is very useful.

To get round this shortage, take some large plastic pots and carefully cut out the base with a Stanley knife. Do be careful though, they're wickedly sharp! Place the pots onto the bag and, using them as a template, cut circular holes into the plastic. Then screw the pots into the bag and fill with the contents of a second grow bag or a decent multi-purpose compost.

These pots will provide enough compost to ensure good plants and the depth to firmly hold plant supporting bamboo canes.

The second problem is getting water and feed into the grow bag when the plants are grown. You can, as I did, buy some little cups that screw into the bag and then you water into these. Having bought these, I realized that small pots with the base cut out will do the same job for a lot less money.

Finally on grow bags, don't forget to make some drainage holes in the grow bag, best about half an inch (1cm) above the bottom. If you don't, the bag can fill with water and drown your plants.

2

SUCCESSIONAL GROWING

The secret to maximizing your crop from a given space and enjoying the fruits of your labour at their best is successional growing. A good example of this would be the lettuce. If you sowed a row of seed directly in place, then the space is going to be tied up for ten weeks while they grow to usable size. Then you would harvest maybe two or three in the week when they're perfect and the rest would bolt making them unusable. Bolting is the term we use to describe a plant going to seed.

With successional growing we start by sowing into modules or small pots each week or two. These are then planted out after three weeks or so and grown on to harvest. This way we use less space for less time and don't waste time and space growing more crops than we need.

Some plants are not suited to this method, basically the root crops like carrots and parsnips as transplanting tends to result in misshaped roots, but for most vegetables it's an effective way of getting more from less.

With the bean family it can take between two and three weeks before the seed germinates so they're well worth starting in pots even if you're not looking for successional crops. The cabbage family may germinate faster but they do take a while to become large enough to need planting in their final spot. If you consider the fact that bean seeds are huge in comparison to the tiny cabbage seed, it makes sense that the bean, once germinated, shoots away whereas the cabbage grows on much more slowly.

Take a seed tray, insert a 15 cell module and fill with multi-purpose compost. Sow four or five seeds in three modules and label with the variety and date. Two weeks later, sow into the next three modules and thin out the first modules to one seedling per module by just pinching off the unwanted seedlings.

Keep an eye on the modules by lifting from the tray and once the roots start to poke through the holes, move the whole module into a 3 inch (8cm) square plastic pot on top of some more compost.

Square pots have an advantage of using all the space when put together in a tray and they stop the roots from going round and round the bottom of the pot. It's probably best to plant out the small container cabbages directly from the 3 inch pots but if there is nowhere to put them you can step up into 5 inch (12cm) pots until space is available.

If you're growing two varieties of cabbage or cabbage and cauliflower, start one variety at one end of the tray and the other from the other side.

The main thing is to use the least space we need to grow the plant on. I've started half a dozen tomatoes off in an old vending machine cup, then transplanted the seedlings on to individual pots before planting out.

When transplanting seedlings, always hold them by the leaves, never by the stem of the plant which is very fragile. Ensure they're well loosened before lifting as it is easy to break the roots as well. You cannot be too gentle with small seedlings.

For plants that need warmth, like the tomato, the window sill is fine although the ultimate has to be a thermostatically controlled electric propagator. You can buy propagators specifically designed to fit on window sills as well.

The cheap electric propagators are OK but, and it's a big but, they have a tendency to cook your seedlings. They have no control and may be fine for a cold evening but when the sun comes out early in the morning the temperature shoots up and you come down to a tray of dead seedlings. You only need to forget once and you'll be cursing not praising your bargain.

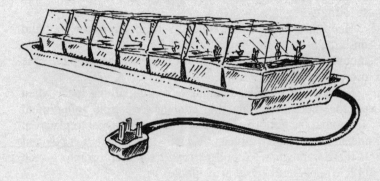

Fig. 7. Window sill propagator.

One answer is to buy a thermostatic control such as those designed for aquariums. The sensor, which should be of a type safe to use in wet conditions, is placed inside the propagator or even in a pot of compost. The control will then automatically switch on and off to maintain the temperature you set.

There are various heating systems you can buy designed for greenhouses ranging from paraffin space heaters to electric soil warming cables to keep a bench warm but they depend on you having a greenhouse, of course. For a coldframe I have tried a small paraffin heater (described as suitable for a coldframe) but the build up of heat above the heater caused the glass to crack.

My favourite propagator has to be my Vitopod. It's a large, heated, height-adjustable propagator, a mini-greenhouse and a cold frame all wrapped up into one. The base tray has a built in electric element controlled by a thermostat so plants never cook. Ventilation is adjustable through side vents and vents in the top but best of all you can increase the height of the

Fig. 8. Vitopod propagator.

propagator by adding another set of side walls. If you're starting plants and the weather changes delaying the time they can go outside, you can hold them under cover for extra weeks in the taller propagator.

One problem with window sills is that the seedlings can become scorched by strong sunlight from south-facing windows and will become drawn and leggy in north-facing situations. It's worth shading if it's a sunny spring; a net curtain works well.

To help stop the seedlings all leaning to the window, take a piece of cardboard and fold it so some is held under the tray and the rest sticks up behind the tray. Fix some aluminium foil to the card and it will reflect light back onto the plants.

Starting those beans and cabbages off under cover will extend your season, once again making best use of your space over time but we don't really want to convert the whole house to a plant nursery.

A greenhouse is ideal but takes up room and the assumption is that you don't have room to spare or you wouldn't be small space growing. The solution is to have a coldframe. First though a word of warning. Glass is always a risk when there are children and pets about. Our cat decided the cold frame was a great stepping stone when she jumped off the flat roof and now only has eight of her nine lives left.

You can buy coldframes made of glass or twinwall plastic; the plastic is, of course, much safer. The plastic doesn't allow so much light through but plastic frames are warmer which seems to balance out.

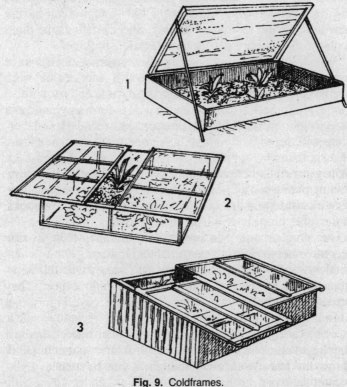

Fig. 9. Coldframes.
(1) Wooden box frame with polythene lid.
(2) Purpose-made aluminium and glass coldframe.
(3) Home-made frame.

There isn't much volume in a coldframe to hold the warmth overnight so insulating with fleece, old net curtains or even newspaper will help to avoid a sharp drop in a frost. The soil will be quite cold in late winter and early spring, so if you can get some sheet polystyrene and lay it on the base you'll keep the coldframe warmer. One good source is electrical appliance retailers who have loads of polystyrene sheets from packing materials they just throw away.

You can build your own coldframe with wooden sides and line the base and sides with polystyrene. Not just warm, the white sheets will reflect light as well which helps the plants grow.

The top can be made from glass. Watch out for someone having double glazing fitted as the old windows can have a new lease of life in your coldframe. Sheet plastic is the thing to use if those pesky pets or children are a problem.

With a little ingenuity you can also construct cloches to fit individual pots and tubs. Take some stiff wire, an old wire coathanger or some thick stiff electrical cable and form into a circle. Fix some thin canes from the wire to form a pyramid and then wrap some flexible clear plastic sheet around. How decorative will depend on your skill. A good source for the plastic sheet is a camping supplies shop where it is sold as groundsheet. With square tubs the construction process is easier as you can use thin strips of wood as the base which is easier to fix the canes to.

With raised beds it's quite easy to form hoops using plastic water pipe cheaply available from builders' merchants. Tie some canes on and then cover with plastic to form a large cloche or net to protect from birds and insects.

Most of the garden centres and DIY stores will sell mini-greenhouses which are better than you might expect. They come with tubular metal frames and the covering is thin plastic sheeting with a zip-up door.

The covers don't tend to last more than three years but they're so cheap to buy that it doesn't matter so much. Don't throw the framework away though, it can be used as light-weight shelving.

You can make your own mini-greenhouse using clear plastic sheeting but the savings against bargain offers available at end of season sales are minimal.

Fig. 10. Mini-greenhouse.

Hardening Off

When we've grown our plant on the nice warm window sill or in the sheltered coldframe, the worst thing we can do is to just plonk it outside. The tender young thing will often just curl up and die. At best it'll suffer a check in growth and take weeks to recover.

You need to get your plant used to the change in conditions over a few days at least. Move from the window sill to the coldframe and after a few days start leaving the lights open in the day. It isn't just the temperature but also the wind that helps to toughen the plant for the ordeals of the big wide world. Some gardeners stroke their plants each day for a week as they feel it helps with the process before putting them into the frame, which seems a bit time-consuming to me.

Next leave the frame open at night and take the plant out of the frame in the day. By the end of a week the new tough plant will cope with the world when you plant it out.

3

COMPOSTS AND FERTILIZERS

When you're growing in pots or tight planted raised beds, you can't just use ordinary garden soil. It won't contain the nutrients your crops need to grow properly in the limited space and is unlikely to drain well enough.

Although plants, like us, need water, just like us they can drown if there's too much.

The roots need some oxygen and keeping them in a pool of water where they exhaust the oxygen means they'll keel over and die.

Compost is one of the most confusing terms in gardening. When used as a verb, as in 'I've composted the kitchen waste', it's a reference to the magical process whereby waste materials are converted to a useful plant food.

When used as a noun, as in 'multi-purpose compost', it describes a multitude of different materials with different properties and is interchangeable with 'growing medium'.

Making Compost

Since we're talking about small space gardening, I'm going to assume you don't have a lot of room for multiple compost bins and the time to turn them over and so on to make your compost.

If you only have a patio or balcony to play with, then really I'd forget about making your own compost. If your council run a green or kitchen waste collection service, then it's better to give it to them to process. If they don't, then ask them why not!

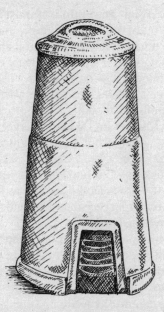

Fig. 11. Plastic barrel type compost bin.

You may have heard about making worm compost, which is an excellent material, but here again it does take up some space and while, in theory, you can have a worm composter in the house, I wouldn't advise it.

In a small garden the easiest and most cost effective way to make your compost is in one of the purpose made bins. They look like a black or green plastic barrel and don't take up much space. You can buy bins designed to look like old fashioned beehives if you don't want a plastic barrel in the garden or do what we do and hide it behind some climbing plants and bushes.

Now the plastic barrel styles come with a little door at the base, which is designed for removing the finished product. It's a great idea but my experience is that they don't work. The compacted compost is just too difficult to excavate from the small doorway. So you need a good couple of square metres by your bin as I'll explain later.

What goes into Compost?

There is a little bit of an art to making compost. It's a matter of balance. Too much of any one material and you can end up with a smelly, soggy mess. But with plenty of variety you end up with a marvellous growing material.

You can add nearly any green garden waste. There are a few things to be careful of though. Avoid diseased material like blighted potato foliage. In a general, large garden compost I wouldn't worry about it but in this tight eco-system we're creating you need to be more careful.

Lawn mowings are fine so long as you haven't used a weedkiller on your lawn. Do be careful, as lots of lawn fertilizers contain a broad leaved plant herbicide and this will kill your crops as well as dandelions.

There is another problem with lawn mowings in that they can compact and so don't rot down. If you can, mix them with some other material. An inch thick layer of lawn clippings followed by some kitchen waste or paper shreddings and then more lawn mowings works well.

Hedge clippings can go into the bin so long as the wood isn't too thick. If you have a garden shredder, run them through that as the smaller pieces will compost in a tenth of the time of large twigs. With light clippings you can spread these onto a lawn and run a hover mower over them. It isn't quite as good as a shredder but does help a lot.

Thick roots and stems will compost better if they're crushed. Brassica stems can just be bashed a few times with a lump hammer to help them break down.

With perennial weeds, such as dandelions or dock leaves, adding them to the heap can be a problem as they start to re-grow. The easy answer is to cut the leaves off, which go straight into the bin, and put the roots into a bucket of water for a couple of weeks and drown them. Tip the water and weed roots into the bin as the water will have absorbed useful minerals from those roots.

Kitchen waste will compost but don't add any meat or fish products whether raw or cooked. These will stink and attract rats. That includes gravy soaked cooked vegetables, by the way.

You can add eggshells, but crush them up. It becomes a

habit after a while, crack the egg and crush the shell into bits as you drop it into the waste bin.

You can add a small amount of shredded paper. Since we've all got to worry about identify theft and are encouraged to shred our bank statements, etc, we have a material that will add well to the compost bin. Paper shreddings are especially useful for balancing lawn mowings.

Cardboard torn up small can go into the bin as well. The brown corrugated type is fine but take off any parcel tape. That stuff seems to have been designed to last forever. Don't use the 'better quality' white or coloured glazed cardboard though, it doesn't seem to rot down.

Do not add any plastic wrapping material, plastic bags, etc. There are some made of compostable material nowadays but unless you're sure they're the right sort then don't. All that will happen is they'll come out as they went in. The same goes for a lot of sweet packets. Why they have to make the wrapper of a Flake last for centuries I don't know but they do.

Never add the contents of the cat litter tray or the dog's business. Both can carry disease and parasites particularly harmful to pregnant women and children.

The Process

Now all you need to do is put the materials into the bin and let nature take its course. Compost is made by the action of two things: microbes and worms. The microbes are everywhere but worms may be in short supply. Place your bin onto bare earth and worms will magically appear.

I have seen people put bins onto concrete and wonder why the compost takes ages and never seems properly rotted down. You may well open the lid and find lots of thin red worms. These are the brandling worms beloved of fishermen and they're working hard for you – eating the waste and converting it in their gut to the finest plant food.

Both worms and microbes need some water to live so don't let your compost bin dry out but don't have it soaking wet either. Just damp is fine. The best way to add water is with a watering can with a rose on it so the water is distributed evenly.

If compost becomes acid, then the microbes cannot operate so well and the worms will move out, so adding a little lime will 'keep it sweet' as we say. Just buy some garden lime (it's very cheap in the old fashioned garden suppliers) and dust over the surface every foot (30cm) or so. When I say dust, think of the icing sugar on a cake. You only need a little. I use an old tablespoonful on each layer for my dustbin sized compost bin.

You can also buy compost accelerators cheaply. Basically these provide additional nitrogen to feed the process. Petrol on the fire. If you use these, and I do, put a sprinkling on after a 6 inch (15cm) layer and then add lime on the next 6 inch layer and so forth.

To avoid things becoming too compact and the materials around the edge not rotting, just use a hand fork to stir around the top layer before adding the next lot of materials.

After some months the bin will have rotted down most of the material in the lower regions. As I said, there is a little door to enable removal of the finished compost but I think the best way is simply to lift the bin up and off the compost.

Then, using a garden fork, take the top partially rotted material off and put aside. Either into a wheelbarrow or onto a sheet is fine. We find old shower curtains do sterling duty as tarpaulins in the garden.

The finished compost at the base can then be used and the partially rotted goes back into the bin to finish rotting down.

Leafmould

Come the autumn the trees lose their leaves which in the forest would just lie on the floor to rot down. However, the tree sucks back most of the nutrients before it discards those leaves so leafmould doesn't contain much in the way of nutrients unlike compost. However, leafmould is a great soil conditioner and can form the base of homemade seed composts.

It's very easy to make, especially if you have one of those leaf vacuums with a built in mulcher. Just pop the leaves into a large bin bag, watering occasionally as you fill it to keep them just damp. When full, tie the bag up and pierce some holes into it – I just poke it a few times with a garden fork.

Place the bag somewhere out of the way, under a hedge or behind the shed and forget it. After a year it's converted into useful leafmould. It couldn't be simpler.

Commercial Composts

How they're made and what to look for
The composts you buy from the garden centre are different from the compost you make yourself. Think of your homemade compost as supplement to the soil or part of a growing medium for pot growing.

Commercial composts tend to be more consistent than homemade compost as they're made in bulk. Often councils collect green waste materials which are composted and form part of the bags you buy.

Because they're dealing with hundreds of tonnes, the green waste is taken to a processor who puts it all through a giant shredder. We're talking about an industrial scale process here.

This shredded material is then stacked in windrows, long piles about 8 feet (2.5 metres) high which quickly heat up and start to rot down. They're an amazing sight, especially in the autumn, with steam rising off them.

They're turned a number of times by JCBs to bring the materials from the outside to the inside and to make sure everything gets heated up and rotted down. This heating process effectively sterilizes the compost, killing any weed seeds, fungal spores and disease microbes.

Once finished, the compost is fed through a giant sieve to remove the larger pieces which are returned to the beginning of the process. Having visited a processor I know that different compost manufacturers have different specifications for their compost. Some insist the holes in the sieve are 20mm and some 40mm. The smaller the better, in this case.

The manufacturer will then take this compost and mix it with peat or a peat substitute and add fertilizer and lime to balance it. The exact mix will vary according to the manufacturer.

As with many things; the more you pay, usually the better the product. If you buy a cheap grow bag and open it up to examine the contents, you'll be amazed at anything growing in there. I've found bits of wood and plastic and even broken glass (so be careful).

A good quality compost should have no large lumps of unrotted material and be pleasant to use. These are often referred to as 'soil less' composts. You'll find a lot of different makes, Humax being one well respected brand although I tend to use my local garden supplier's own brand product which is superb. Buy a bag and see what you think is my best advice.

You can buy compost especially for seed, which has a finer consistency and lower level of nutrients or a multi-purpose, more general compost. For most things I only bother with multi-purpose potting compost.

You can also buy ericaceous compost which is lime free and designed for acid hating plants.

John Innes Composts

John Innes was a nineteenth century property and land dealer in the City of London. On his death in 1904 he bequeathed his fortune and estate to the improvement of horticulture by experiments and research which resulted in the establishment of the John Innes Institute, now part of the John Innes Centre.

The Institute developed some standard formulas for composts based on loam. Loam is made by stacking turves upside down for six months to rot down the grass. The benefit of using loam is that it contains small particles of clay which have the capacity to absorb and release plant nutrients as required by the plants.

The loam is sieved and sterilized before being used. You can, I believe, still buy steam soil sterilizers and I've heard of people sterilizing small quantities in the kitchen microwave. I've not tried this myself as the word divorce came into the conversation about it.

To this base of loam, peat is added to increase the water retaining capacity and lighten the mixture along with coarse sand to help drainage. Finally, fertilizer is added along with lime to balance the acidity.

You may hear people talk about John Innes number one or number three. The number refers to the exact mixture used as laid down by the Institute.

John Innes Seed Compost is for sowing seeds in and contains a low level of nutrients, just some superphosphate and lime.

John Innes Cutting Compost is for cuttings and contains no added fertilizer.

John Innes Potting Compost No. 1 is for young seedlings and has a low level of general nutrients.

John Innes Potting Compost No. 2 is often used for house plants and some vegetables containing double the amount of nutrients in No. 1.

John Innes Potting Compost No. 3 is for the greedier vegetables and shrubs, etc, being the richest mixture.

John Innes Potting Ericaceous Compost is acid, containing no lime, and is ideal for acid loving plants such as blueberries.

Most things will grow perfectly well in standard good-quality multi-purpose compost but I found you can get the best performance by suiting the growing medium to the plant and adding a few extras.

With all commercial composts the quality deteriorates in store. Often they're kept outside and the bags have small holes that allow water in and nutrients to wash out. The worst time to buy is the end of the year as the stock has been sitting around all season. The best time to buy is when the new stock arrives. Store protected from rain and you'll have better results.

Lime

Most compost is geared for flowers and so slightly acid. Vegetables need lots of nutrients and acid tends to hinder their take up of these so I like to add a little lime except for erica-ceous plants and potatoes. The potato seems to prefer a pH of around 5.5 to 6.0 and ericaceous fruits like cranberries actually like their soil pH as low as 4.5. The acidity of soil is measured on the pH scale. 1 to 7 is acid and 7 and above alkaline or chalky. The general range you find soil in is between 5.00 and 8.00. You can buy testing kits fairly cheaply from the garden centres and DIY stores, but you really don't need to worry too much; it's growing not rocket science. The one vegetable group that really benefits from lime is the brassica (cabbage) family who like their soil neutral with a pH of 7.00. Most other vegetables like 6.00 to 6.5.

For general vegetables I use a tablespoon of garden lime to a 2 gallon (9 litre) bucket of standard multi-purpose compost.

Vermiculite and Perlite
These are mineral products that lighten the compost, improving drainage and assisting water penetration if the compost should dry out.

Sand
Some crops like carrots prefer a sandy soil and so I add sharp or concrete making sand. Just buy a bag from the DIY or builders' merchants. Not to be confused with horticultural sand that costs a fortune!

Water Retaining Gel Crystals
These are bought in packs and arrive as little crystals that swell tremendously when they get wet. Growing in pots means there is very little reservoir of water available for plants and if you miss a day in hot weather your plants can be ruined. Adding these to the compost means you build in a safety margin and even things out, which gives better crops.

Non-woody plants hold themselves up by using water pressure within the plant. That's why thirsty plants fold over and wilt. When this happens it damages the internal cell structure of the plant, making it more susceptible to fungal and other disease infection. The more frequently the plant dries and wilts, the greater the risk of infection.

Tomatoes really don't like drying out at any stage and it results in problems ranging from cracked skins to blossom end rot where the base of the tomato turns black and rots. Because they're such a thirsty plant though, water crystals will not buy you much time.

Fertilizers

To be healthy, we need a diet with protein, carbohydrate and vitamins. Plants are similar except that they need NPK and micro-nutrients.

N is Nitrogen which is needed for the production of leaves. So plants like lettuce or cabbage that we grow for the leaves need more nitrogen.

P is Phosphorus which is used for roots. Plants such as carrots and parsnips where we grow them for the roots need lots of phosphorus.

K is for Potassium (commonly called potash, it has the chemical symbol K from its Latin name kalium) which is used for flower and fruit production.

The micro-nutrients are minerals like magnesium and iron. They only need tiny amounts but they do need them to thrive.

When you buy fertilizers you will see numbers on the packet that refer to the strength of the fertilizer and the balance. 5:5:5 means basically 5 per cent of each of the major groups whereas 5:10:10 means a fertilizer high in phosphorus and potassium.

You can get them as a dry material which is applied to the soil and gradually dissolves. Fish, blood and bone is a balanced NPK fertilizer as is the inorganic Growmore. I prefer the fish, blood and bone as it dissolves more slowly and spreads its effect over a longer period. However, it can cause pet cats and dogs to show great interest in your soil and start digging things up.

For long-term fertilizer used in pots you need a controlled release fertilizer. The best known brands are Osmacote and Miracle-Gro. The nutrients are pelleted and release slowly and evenly over a period of six months, about enough to get your plants through the main season.

With feeding pot grown plants through the season we use liquid feeds of which there are three basic types:

General Plant Fertilizer – usually high in nitrogen and therefore best for leafy vegetables.

Tomato Feed – higher in phosphorus and potash. Not only for use on tomatoes but good for root and fruit crops.

Ericaceous Feed – especially for the lime hating plants.

These can come as a liquid or in the form of granules to mix with water. Try to apply them directly to the soil rather than over the leaves of the plant.

Now when you buy fertilizers, especially tomato fertilizer for some reason, you'll see there's a wide range of prices for similar sized bottles. If you check the packets you'll see that some are twice as strong as others so you need to use less. Those NPK numbers I mentioned above.

The better quality manufacturers also add micro-nutrients and trace elements like magnesium which does make a difference. I'm very frugal but sometimes you can be penny wise and pound foolish.

Specific Compost Mixes

Raised Beds

For growing in raised beds at the end of each year spread a couple of inches of your own compost and any leafmould you have made onto the surface and then lightly fork into the top 6 inches (15cm).

The worms will then help you by pulling this deeper into the soil. If you haven't got homemade compost, use some cheap multi-purpose compost (bought in the large 300 litre bags) the same way. If you're pot growing as well, the old spent compost from the pots can go onto the raised beds.

Add about 100g per square metre (4 oz per 10.8 square feet) of general fertilizer like fish, blood and bone or Growmore to provide a good base.

Every fourth year in January or February spread about 200g per square metre (8 oz per 10.8 square feet) of garden lime and let the weather wash it into the soil. If you have a pH tester, you are aiming for a pH of around 6.0.

General Pot and Container Growing

For most pot growing you can just use multi-purpose compost with a little lime added as above and some water retaining gel crystals. Slightly better is to add 1 part John Innes No. 3 to 3 parts multi-purpose soil-less compost by volume.

Carrots and Parsnips

These root crops like a sandy soil and the show growers grow them in barrels and regularly produce roots taller than me! For home grown table carrots a mix of 70:30 by volume of multi-purpose compost and sharp sand is adequate or 3 parts multi-purpose compost, 2 parts John Innes and 1 part sharp (concrete) sand to produce the best results. The latter mix is also good for herbs.

To every 10 litres (17½ pints) or so of compost mix, add 25g (1 oz) of general purpose fertilizer like fish, blood and bone or Growmore for carrots.

Brassica Mix

Brassicas (the cabbage family) are greedy plants and need a lot of nitrogen to form their leaves. When growing in the soil they will often fail to perform if the wind rocks the plant and breaks the tiny hairs on the roots that take in nutrients from the soil.

They much prefer a firm soil so the best growing medium is John Innes No. 3 to which additional lime has been added. Add some slow release fertilizer granules (as per the instructions on the pack) as well as liquid feeding.

Potato Mix

Show growers always grow their perfect specimens in bags using a mixture of peat with added fertilizer. They all have their own mixes and quantities of fertilizer to add but for table growing you'll get good results just using a multi-purpose compost with added slow release fertilizer and 1 part vermiculite to 5 parts compost by volume to lighten the mix. Add a specific potato fertilizer as per the instructions but do not add lime to this mix as potatoes like a lower pH than other vegetables. Add about 70g (2.5 oz) of calcified seaweed to each 10 litres (17½ pints) of compost to provide some micronutrients.

Herb Mix

Herbs most often come from the Mediterranean region and grow on sandy soils low in nutrients. We find that the best mix is multi-purpose compost mixed with leafmould and sharp sand in equal measure by volume or 2 parts multi-purpose compost to 1 part sand. If the mix feels a little solid, add some fine grit or vermiculite to open it up a little more.

Replacing Compost

The nutrients in commercial composts will last about six weeks and thereafter you'll be adding fertilizer to keep your plants growing. However, they won't use up all the nutrients and, over time, these will become unbalanced. If you use terracotta pots you can even see the salts from excess nutrients and tap water start to appear on the outside.

It's perfectly safe to use exhausted compost as a soil conditioner in a garden and if you're growing on a balcony check out your gardening friends who can make good use of it.

With permanent bushes in pots it's a good idea to replace some of the compost every couple of years. Leave it until they are dormant in winter and allow them to get quite dry. Remove from the pot and shake and knock as much compost off the rootball as you can without causing damage to the roots. Then pot back up with fresh compost.

4

SEEDS AND/OR PLANTS

One annoyance for the small scale grower is the number of seeds in a packet. If you only want half a dozen cabbages a year, a packet containing 400 seeds seems a little excessive.

However, not every seed will germinate and grow into a plant. Germination rates vary according to the age of the seed and how they've been kept, but even at 50 per cent germination rate, that's still theoretically 200 cabbages from a packet. Usually with small seeds you sow a few and then select the best seedlings to grow on so now we're down to about 80 cabbages from the packet. So it's not quite as bad as it seems at first glance, although that's still 12 years' supply.

Luckily you don't have to use all your seeds in one go. Most seeds can be stored for a number of years as long as you keep them properly. The three main points are to keep the seeds cool, but not frozen, dark, dry and to exclude air. Reseal the little silver foil packets by folding over and then place the seeds in an airtight tin or plastic storage box. Ideally you would keep them in the fridge but anywhere cool will have to suffice in most households.

If you have some of those little sachets of silica gel desiccant that often come with electronic equipment to keep it dry, pop a few in with your seeds to soak up any moisture in the air. You can 're-charge' the packets if needed by putting them on a hot radiator or in a very low oven for half an hour.

The chart on page 58 will give you some guidance on lifespan but seeds can really surprise you by being viable well beyond what is expected. You will see there is usually a 'sow by' date on the packet. Just like food manufacturers with their 'use by' dates, seed merchants are cautious.

Even when past their best, you'll find that some of the seeds will germinate although the percentage falls year on year. You can test the viability of stored seeds by chitting. To chit, your seeds need to think they've been sown, so take a piece of kitchen roll and dampen it. Onto the damp kitchen roll put a number of seeds (20 is good if you have a lot), and place into a plastic bag or Tupperware type container. Put into somewhere dark and warm, such as an airing cupboard or a closed cupboard in an occupied room.

Check the seeds to see which have sprouted; if they fail, you haven't wasted time and effort planting them. The table on page 58 gives the average germination time for each seed, so you know how long to wait before declaring a failure. Often they germinate well before the average time, so check frequently.

There are some seed suppliers specializing in small quantities but, as a rule, I don't think they are worth it. As I said above, the actual number of plants to seeds can be as low as 20 per cent and the seeds will store.

Because the quality of seeds can vary, I would always advise buying directly from reputable, established seed suppliers. Bargain offers from unknown companies on the internet can often turn out to be very false economy – even when they actually deliver.

It's easy enough to buy from garden centres and super-markets but the choice is limited compared to the seed merchants' catalogues and the condition the seeds have been kept in will make a huge difference to germination rates. A season on the shelves in a garden centre using greenhouses as buildings will have heated and cooled the seeds a few times plus moisture may have penetrated the pack if they're not in sealed foil. That treatment can seriously lower the germina-tion rate.

Besides, it's a lovely way to spend a few winter evenings making lists of seeds from catalogues and then realizing you need a farm to grow all you fancy so trimming the list down.

When choosing your seeds from catalogues look out for expressions like 'suitable for close spacing' or 'mini-vegetable'.

These are usually the types that can be container grown. With the growth in interest in container growing, some seed merchants are starting to have specialist sections in their catalogues as well.

One final point on choosing among the bewildering array of varieties available is to look for the RHS Award of Garden Merit. Awards are given after a period of trial at an RHS garden and judged by the Royal Horticultural Society's Standing and Joint Committees. Committees draw upon the knowledge and experience of a wide range of members, including nurserymen, specialist growers, and well-known horticulturists.

The RHS states that for a plant to be awarded the coveted Award of Garden Merit it should comply with the following criteria:

Must be of outstanding excellence for ordinary garden decoration or use

Must be readily available

Must be of good constitution

Must not require highly specialist growing conditions or care

Must not be particularly susceptible to any pest or disease

Must not be subject to an unreasonable degree of reversion in its vegetative or floral characteristics

Accordingly, they're particularly easy for the new grower and, given a choice between similar varieties, go for the one with the Award.

When buying seeds you may come across pelleted seed. Here the seeds are individually covered with a coating that contains anti-fungal compounds and a little fertilizer. The germination rate of pelleted seed is high, often near 100 per cent and they are easier to handle. However, they're more expensive to buy so you win with one hand and lose with the other.

You'll often come across the term hybrid or F1 which seems to be a source of confusion. Breeders discovered that if you crossed two varieties, say one with good flavour and another with disease resistance the resulting offspring would have the best of both parents along with something known as hybrid vigour. They would grow much better than either of their parents.

Unfortunately, the plants bred from those offspring didn't come true to their parent so F1 seeds have to be re-created each time. Some organic growers don't like F1 varieties because of the fact they cannot save seed from them. Producing F1 seeds is really a task for the seed merchant. Usually F1 varieties are well worth the extra cost of the seeds.

Don't forget another source of seeds and plants – friends. I often find myself with plants left over that I've started from seed, not to mention half packets of this and that seed I'm trialing. It just feels plain wrong to throw away a plant because I've had more success than expected and I'd much rather give it away to someone who will benefit. Don't forget to give the pots back (washed) though!

If you join a local horticultural club or one of the National Vegetable Society's district associations, you'll soon be meeting up with like minded growers and swapping seeds and plants along with help and information.

The alternative to starting from seed is to buy young plants for growing on from a nursery or garden centre. The advantage to this is that you can get good quality plants without the bother of sowing, transplanting and possibly wasting seeds but the drawback is that your choice is limited to what they have in stock and you'll pay more for a couple of plants than an entire packet of seeds.

Do check the quality carefully though. As vegetable growing has become a trendy bandwagon, some garden centres think they can get away with very inferior stock. I've also found that labels can end up being swapped so you don't get the variety you expect.

There is another problem to using plants in that the timing is controlled by someone else. They're in stock for a limited time and so successional planting and cropping is well nigh impossible.

One exception to this (there's always one!) is tomato plants. If you just buy one plant and allow some side shoots to develop to a few inches long, then you can take those off and

just plant them at half their depth into 3 inch (8cm) pots of
very damp compost.

Don't put them into too sunny a place and they'll quickly
root and start growing. You only need to buy one plant per
variety to get as many plants as you could want.

These later plants will be behind your first one but not as far
behind as you might expect. I always take some side shoots
for additional plants later in the year anyway.

Seed Life Chart

Seed	Expected (Life Years)	Avg Days to Germination
Beans, Broad	2	21
Beans, French	2	14
Beans, Runner	2	14
Beetroot	5	13
Spinach Beet, Chards	5	13
Broccoli	5	8
Cabbage	5	8
Carrot	3	16
Cauliflower	5	8
Cucumber	7	9
Kale	4	8
Kohlrabi	4	7
Leek	3	14
Lettuce	4	7
Marrow and Courgettes	6	7
Onion	4	14
Parsley	2	10
Parsnip	1	17
Peas	2	10
Radish	4	6
Salsify	2	12
Spinach	2	11
Swede	2	8
Sweetcorn	3	9
Tomato	3	7
Turnip	2	8

5

TOOLS AND WATER

Apart from an ordinary garden fork and spade if creating raised beds, the small space gardener needs very little in the way of tools and the pot grower even less.

For pot growing I would suggest you can get away at a pinch with just one narrow trowel but the ideal wish list is a little longer. In addition to the narrow trowel, a wider trowel is useful for larger plants.

I've never found too much use for a hand fork but the double hoe cultivator with a blade on one side and a fork on the other is extremely handy as a cultivator for fluffing up the soil and as a hoe for drawing shallow trenches and weeding.

Fig. 12. Wolf double hoe.

The tools with interchangeable handles like the Wolf range are particularly useful when dealing with raised beds as you can attach a longer handle, which means you can avoid bending or getting on your knees so much. For those with limited mobility working on a bench bed, the intermediate size could be just the ticket.

For those suffering lack of grip due to arthritis, etc, there are hand tools sold under the brand Easi-Grip where the handle is at 90 degrees to the tool, enabling the force line to pass in a straight line through the wrist and arm and reducing stress, especially when twisting. Joseph Bentley have some similar pistol grip hand trowels available.

You might be able to make an argument for a bulb planter if you are planting out a large number of plants but otherwise I'm hard pressed to think of any other tools you actually would need and will not end up left in the store cupboard as they're more trouble than they're worth.

Whatever tools you do buy, buy quality. Cheap sets with trowel and fork for a pound or even 50p may seem a bargain but when the blade is rusty and the fork's tines have bent up a few months later you'll be replacing them. Decent tools last a life-time – or longer. My favourite hoe is two years older than I am!

Being a sucker for gadgets, I have tried a number of devices that claim to make sowing seeds easier but for small seeds I still rely on a pencil. Lick the end of the pencil and dip into the seeds where it will pick one or two up for you. The blunt end doubles as a dibber for small holes when transplanting and my finger is the perfect tool for larger holes.

One 'gadget' I would not be without though is a plastic potting tidy tray. If you're growing on a balcony and have to pot in the house, then the tray keeps the composts from ending up all over the floor.

For measuring when mixing composts I use either a large pot or a bucket for bigger quantities, and an old set of scales is useful for measuring fertilizers although I still contend that the kitchen scales are fine when washed out!

Some equipment for watering plants, especially when growing a lot in pots, is worth consideration. A good capacity, 10 or 12 litre watering can will save a lot of time going back and forth compared to a 7 litre can. Watering plants to the rear in a group of pots can be difficult and the answer here is simply to use a can with a longer spout.

Fig. 13. Potting tray.

When you have a lot of pots and the weather is hot, watering can become a real chore. If you have an outside tap, then consider a drip irrigation system. These can be very expensive but shop around. All they really consist of is a fitting to go on the tap, a narrow hose, various joining and T splitting pieces and drip ends. Some good garden supply stores, as against those retail emporiums calling themselves garden centres, will sell the parts separately. This can be a third of the price of brand name kits. You can even get a computer controlled tap that can be programmed to allow water to flow for a number of hours a day. I suppose it would help if you were away for a week but hopefully you have a neighbour who could do the same in return for a few tomatoes.

With raised beds and borders in hot weather a hosepipe will save hours but before you start squirting away, check they really do need watering. Wilting plants is an obvious sign you need to water, and quickly, but just because the surface of the soil is dry doesn't mean it is time to water.

I use my Mark 1 water meter, also known as my index

finger. Insert into the soil and if it is dry below an inch, then it is time to water but often you will find it is actually quite moist below the surface.

When you do water, water properly. This applies to lawns and decorative borders as well as to a vegetable plot. A quick sprinkle will wet the surface but not sink far into the soil and this means the roots will seek out the moisture at the surface. Roots that have gone down are cushioned against quick changes in weather and damage but surface roots are weak and vulnerable to damage.

With watering, 'little and often' is absolutely the wrong thing for established plants. Watering thoroughly every three or four days with sufficient to soak down below the surface will do your plants far more good.

Slow watering is better than fast as well; it allows time for the water to trickle down and get into all the minute channels between the particles in the soil. Standing with a hosepipe trickling slowly for hours on end is about as exciting as watching paint dry so I use seep hoses. These are porous hosepipes that allow water to seep out in small droplets and slowly soak into the soil.

They will water to about 2 feet (just over half a metre) to each side so they are ideal for raised beds and borders. Just run one hose up the centre of the bed. You can just lay them on the surface but they're more effective if buried just a couple of inches under the ground.

Different makes will tend to seep at different rates so the first time you use a seep hose you'll need to find out how long your set up takes to water your bed properly. After this you'll just turn the hose on and come back three or four or however many hours later and switch off.

It's a sad fact that the usual British summer is more like a monsoon but every so often we get a scorcher and it's inevitably accompanied by a hosepipe ban. There's no ban on using saved rainwater though. You can get a huge range of tubs to store rainwater and diverter kits that attach to the downspout from the gutters to fill them. If space is at a premium you can get slimline water butts that take up little room against a wall.

Plants tend to prefer rainwater to tapwater, especially the ericaceous plants, so they're a sensible investment even if we don't have a hosepipe ban. Another benefit of water butts is that the water is around air temperature whereas tap water is around 5°C even in the summer.

Just like us, plants find it quite a shock to step into a freezing cold shower and, for the plants at least, there's no health benefit! With seedlings and young plants still in a coldframe or on a window sill, the shock can actually kill them. You'll be reducing the temperature of the compost drastically and quickly.

For watering seedlings, keep a small can filled with water either in the coldframe or in the room for window sill plants and use that. Generally it takes about three hours for tapwater to come to room temperature.

Seedlings, like any babies, are delicate and a full size can flooding and knocking them down with the flow isn't good for them. For these use a houseplant small watering can or, better still, buy a fine brass rose to put on the end of your watering can's spout. With the oval shaped roses, turn it so it faces upwards and, when you pour, the water flow will be more gentle.

There are a couple of devices I would recommend to help with watering. The first is a Big Drippa. This is a micro-irrigation drip system with a bag which holds water to feed the system. If you haven't got mains water available, you can simplify the watering by just filling the bag, which saves a lot of time.

The second is the Iroso Water Spike. This is such a clever idea you wonder why it's not been around for years. It is, as the name suggests, a spike you insert into compost next to your plants with a water bottle attached. It works with most plastic water bottles and you can adjust the flow rate to suit your needs. It's great if you're going away for a few days and want to keep some seedlings in pots safely watered.

There are lots of other devices available to help with watering, but those are two I can personally vouch for.

Don't forget with pots and hanging baskets that the roots take up a fair percentage of the storage space available for

Fig. 14. Water spike.

water. The water retaining gel crystals will help but in hot sunny weather you may well need to water twice a day. A good soaking until the water actually drips out through the drainage holes will ensure the whole of the pot, and therefore the root system, has water available.

You may read instructions not to water on a sunny day as the droplets on the leaves will act as magnifying glasses and scorch the leaves. I can't say that I have actually seen this happen – on days that warm the water has evaporated too quickly – but, in any case, try to water the soil not the leaves. It's better to water in the sun than leave the plant to wilt as you wait for sundown.

6

PESTS AND PROBLEMS

One of the benefits of growing in small spaces is that you tend to pay more attention to the individual plants and so pick up on problems as they start when they're easier to resolve. With container growing you also have the advantage of being free of soil borne disease like club-root or onion white rot and 'soil sickness' which is where the same crop is grown for a number of years in the same spot. This depletes and unbalances the available nutrients in the soil.

Slugs and Snails

These really are the worst pest any gardener has to cope with. It seems that no sooner have you got rid of one lot, another lot moves in. If you managed to clear every single slug from your garden, in six weeks you would be back at square one. Not only would they have trekked in from neighbouring gardens but eggs would have hatched. Strangely even hanging baskets aren't immune to the little monsters. We once joked that they must have a parachute brigade but the truth is they will climb walls and down the chain into the basket. That's assuming there were no eggs in the compost.

The easiest answer for slugs in the garden has to be slug pellets but these are a concern to many people in that they contain a chemical called metaldehyde that is poisonous to pets and children. There is also a concern that the dying slug or snail will be eaten by a bird or hedgehog and thereby poison it. Although there is no real evidence of the danger to wildlife being actual rather than theoretical, the poisoning risk to children and pets is there. Most pellets in the UK contain a repellent but any cat or dog owner will tell you how daft they can be and no parent wants to take the risk.

There are now organically approved pellets on the market that are pet and wildlife safe. The active ingredient is ferric phosphate, also called ferramol and they're sold as Advanced Slug Killer by Growing Success. I think they're actually more effective than the conventional type being less likely to dissolve if it rains. They don't so much poison the slugs as stop them from feeding so I suppose the slugs just starve to death. Any pellets not eaten are eventually returned to the soil after being broken down by micro organisms into iron and phosphate. In cost terms they're more expensive but one tub is enough to cover 40 square metres for a season.

There are other methods for dealing with slugs and snails. Nematodes are very effective but I'd suggest they are better for larger plots than for just one small raised bed. You can creep out at dusk with a torch when the slugs break cover to eat your plants and hunt them individually. You'll definitely catch slugs this way but it feels like trying to hold back the tide. Traps containing beer will catch them but you have to dispose of the rotting corpses, which isn't pleasant at all.

Various things can be effective as barriers to slugs. Sharp fine gravel and crushed egg shells may stop them from crossing and you can buy various materials to do the same job.

With pots you can buy copper tape that you apply to the pot. The copper combined with the slime produced by slugs and snails causes them an electric shock so they supposedly won't cross the tape. You can also apply Vaseline or even spray WD40 oil in a circle around the pot to form a barrier.

Personally I've not a lot of faith in barriers; slugs always seem to get through one way or another.

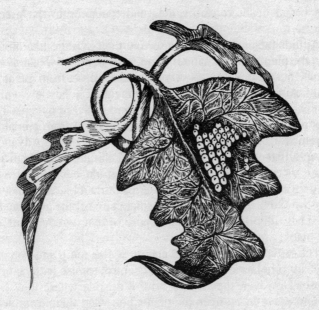

Fig. 15. Caterpillar eggs on leaf.

Caterpillars

Butterflies are beautiful but the caterpillar is a real pest of brassicas. The best method is to prevent the butterflies from laying their eggs in the first place using fine netting or fleece.

The next best is to check under the leaves each day for groups of eggs and just rub them off. These will be seen as small (approximately 2mm) yellow or white spheres often in very regular geometric patterns. You do need to check regularly. It's amazing how quickly the eggs turn into a ravening hoard of caterpillars and then all you have left are skeletons where once there were cabbages. If they have developed into caterpillars, pick them off by hand. Don't worry; they don't bite you!

Aphids

The aphid family of some 500 species includes greenfly and blackfly. It causes damage to numerous plants from cabbages and broad beans to aubergines and tomatoes in the greenhouse.

Aphids feed on plants by inserting their syringe-like mouth into the plants and sucking the sap. This not only weakens the plants but also helps to spread viral disease from plant to plant. Aphids produce a sticky waste called honeydew which forms a growth medium for moulds and is prized by ants. The ants actually farm the aphids and protect them from predators in return for this food.

Aphids tend to concentrate on the lush, growing tip of the plant; too much nitrogen fertilizer will produce just the growth they love. Broad beans always seem to attract blackfly and the best way to dispose of these pests is to clip off the growing tip once it's fully developed and dispose of that together with all the blackfly on it.

The ladybird is the natural enemy of the aphid and you can buy ladybird larvae as a biological control for use in the greenhouse. However, they are of no use outside where they will simply move away from the plants you want them to protect. The best solution outside is simply to wash the aphids off using a water spray or, more effectively, with insecticidal soft soap.

Another method is to provide some sacrificial plants like nasturtiums to attract the aphids away from the crops. I've doubts about the effectiveness of this method as they breed so quickly I think you just end up providing another food source and a reservoir of more pests. Some people swear it works though.

Whitefly

Brassicas are commonly affected by whitefly although the pest does not actually cause much damage to the plants. When you disturb the leaves, a cloud of the small flies may appear. If you think they are harming your crop or causing a nuisance, treat as aphids.

They can be more of a pest in a greenhouse or under cover. In these circumstances you can hang yellow sticky cards between the plants. For some reason the whitefly is attracted to yellow and when it lands on the card it sticks and dies.

Spidermite

The red spidermite is just half a millimetre across and often hard to spot with the naked eye. The leaf damage it causes is usually the first thing noticed. Leaves become bronzed, wither and die. Use a magnifying glass to check if spidermites are the cause: you're looking for tiny red or yellow spiders. A specific biological control, *Phytoseiulus persimilis*, is available but only of use in a greenhouse. Outdoors washing with insecticidal soap is moderately effective. Usually a few are not too damaging but heavy infestations require action to avoid significant crop damage.

Blight

Potato blight (see Potatoes, page 94) isn't usually a problem when growing early potatoes in pots unless you are very unlucky. Unfortunately blight also affects tomatoes and this is quite likely to be a problem if you're not growing under cover.

The spores of the mould *Phytophthora infestans* float in from miles around when the weather is warm and humid and land on your tomato plants. The first sign is small brown patches on the leaves but in as little as a day the whole plant can be affected and dying. The chances are that any tomatoes developing on the plants will be affected and inedible as well.

The first line of defence is to prevent the spores from getting onto the crop, which is why greenhouse crops are rarely bothered. Even partial cover is protection; if you keep the rain off, then the blight is probably kept off.

If you spot blight starting on the leaves, then immediately removing them may save the day but, to be honest, the chances are not good.

You can get various fungicidal sprays for blight which are most effective if applied as a preventative before it strikes. Sometimes fungicides can rescue the situation if applied at the first sign of trouble, but you have to be really fast. Blight spreads incredibly quickly and hours make a big difference.

The traditional spray was Bordeaux mixture. This isn't such a good idea in my opinion as it contains copper and that is hardly good for your diet although it is organically approved.

Inorganic Dithane 945 is effective as long as it is applied before blight has hold, but once again you are adding a chemical residue to your diet.

Rather than spray, once the blight has struck I remove any reasonably developed tomatoes and store them so they are not touching. The green ones will ripen up (see Tomatoes, page 100). Dispose of the plants in the council green waste bin.

7

VEGETABLES

While it's perfectly possible in theory to grow any and every vegetable in a container, if you have a large enough container, not every vegetable is really practical for small space growing. It also makes more sense to concentrate on those vegetables that provide a good return for the space they utilize.

Accordingly, I'm going to concentrate on the vegetables that can be practically grown in a small space and give a reasonable return for the effort. One temptation that growers have is to try everything. Seed and plant catalogues are carefully crafted to sell – mouthwatering flavour, easy to grow, improved and delicious. You may be ready to buy before you even know what the crop is!

I know it sounds very basic, but only grow those vegetables you really like. Having come across a grower who had four varieties of Brussels sprouts on his plot, I said he must really like them. His answer was no, he hated sprouts but they looked so good in the catalogue.

For growing in small spaces and containers, select varieties from the catalogues that state 'suitable for close spacing' or 'mini-vegetable'. I've mentioned varieties but there are new ones introduced each year and old ones dropped so you may not be able to find my suggestions.

My advice would be to start with the salad crops; lettuce and leaves, spring onions, tomatoes and cucumbers as these are the crops where the benefit of freshness is most apparent. Then to grow strawberries as you just can't beat a strawberry straight off the plant but keep the children away from them or you'll never know! Potatoes are another crop well worth patio growing. Yes, you can buy potatoes cheaply in the shops but the flavour of new potatoes harvested an hour before is far superior to anything you can buy.

Artichoke

There are two plants that confusingly share the name artichoke, despite being totally unrelated. The Jerusalem artichoke is grown for the knobbly potato style roots and the globe artichoke for the bulbous flower heads.

Neither is a good prospect for small spaces. The Jerusalem artichoke produces masses of foliage reaching 8 feet (2.5 metres) in height for a few pounds of tubers and if planted in a border effectively becomes a permanent feature, growing back the next year from any small tubers missed when digging them out.

The globe artichoke is a member or the thistle family and produces a very large plant that will dominate a circle 5 feet (1.5 metres) in diameter. They are stunning to look at and can provide an architectural centre point for a decorative garden but very little crop for an awful lot of space.

Asparagus

Asparagus is a crop only available over a short season that takes three years to come into full production and needs a minimum of a 10' x 4' (3m x 1.2m) bed to provide enough to be worthwhile. Because it is also a shallow rooted and delicate plant, underplanting is not feasible and so you tie up a lot of space for little return. I know it's delicious, but not one for the small space gardener.

Aubergine

Aubergines are really a glass house crop in the UK. I've seen them described as suitable for patio growing but I'd say that's only accurate in the sunny south in a good year. If you can provide cover – a plastic tent cloche is fine – then aubergines are worthwhile.

Start from seed in late February or early March in a heated propagator or window sill propagator then move on into 3 inch (8cm) pots when large enough to handle. Keep them indoors in a sunny window until the weather warms up. Finally move up into 8 inch (20cm) pots and feed with tomato feed when the fruits start to develop.

When the flowers appear, mist spraying will encourage the fruit to set. They're not large plants and the weight of the fruits can cause the stems to break so support by tying onto short bamboo stakes.

They are fairly easy, so long as you can keep them warm but they do attract whitefly and aphids which can be a real problem. Red mite can also be a problem with aubergines, but mist spraying seems to deter them and they don't cause a lot of damage.

One word of warning: the stems develop small spines as they mature which can get under the skin and irritate so you may like to wear gloves when handling them.

There's a wide range of varieties: Rosanna, Bonica, Orlando 5 and Calliope being especially dwarf and suitable for small spaces. Having said that, go for the variety you like the flavour of as they're all suitable for pot growing. My favourite for the kitchen is the traditional Black Beauty.

Broad Beans

Broad beans usually need a fair amount of space and whether to grow them will depend on how much you like them. Since they're my favourite vegetable, I admit to some bias here.

For your money, the best variety to grow is undoubtedly 'The Sutton'. It's a dwarf bean, has the RHS Award of Garden Merit, which is always a good indicator, and can be successfully grown in containers.

Sow directly in the final position in March through to July for successional crops. If you can provide some protection against the weather with a cloche, then November to February sowings will provide early crops.

Normally broad beans are grown in double rows with a spacing of 8 inches (20cm) apart each way and 24 inches (just over half a metre) between the double rows. I'd put a double row in a border or raised bed and then underplant up to the row with other crops once they've grown about 9 inches (22cm) high.

In pots, try and use larger pots, so you can get at least six plants per pot. You can get away with 6 inch (15cm) spacing. They're insect pollinated and I've found a lonely single plant can have spotty pod development.

Broad beans, like most legumes, don't need a lot of nitrogen as they produce their own from nodules on the roots but they are potash hungry. In containers, feed with tomato feed for best results.

Dwarf French Beans

Dwarf French beans are ideal for pot growing and will happily edge a decorative border in the garden. Canzone has a particularly compact structure and does well in close spacings or pots but I'd recommend the teepee varieties. These come in green, yellow and purple podded types. The purple are very striking and decorative when in fruit although they sadly turn dark green when cooked. With the teepee varieties, the beans hang outside the foliage. This not only makes picking easier but makes them look attractive.

They're fairly fast growing so usually sown in the final position but they can be started in 3 inch (8cm) pots and transplanted as space becomes available. As with all the bean family, tomato feed is best as they don't need a lot of nitrogen.

French Climbing Beans and Runner Beans

All the climbing beans offer a brilliant return on the small amount of space they take up. They need canes or netting to climb and are a pretty and productive way to hide a fence in the summer, the painted lady runner bean being the most decorative.

Fig. 16. Dwarf French beans.

Fig. 17. Runner beans climbing a fence.

Climbing beans will easily reach 8 feet (2.5 metres) but usually you pinch out the tops when they get to the top of their canes, which encourages them to bush out and produce more beans lower down.

They're very sensitive to frost and usually don't go out into the garden until May or when the last frosts have passed in your area. They can be sown directly but I'd recommend starting singly in 3 inch (8cm) pots and planting out 9 inches (22cm) apart. If you are growing them on a wigwam of canes, then space the canes at that in a circle.

The problem with growing climbing and runner beans in containers is that they require a lot of water. If you think about it, they've a lot of foliage and will, therefore, lose a lot through transpiration from the leaves.

I've successfully grown a wigwam of runner beans in a very large tub, about 4 feet (1.2 metres) in diameter and 3 feet (1 metre) deep but I've also seen them grown in 7 inch (18cm) pots. (The ex-flower tubs I mentioned on page 28 are ideal.) To cope with their water demands, especially when fully grown, in pots consider a drip irrigation system or be prepared to water twice a day, three times in hot weather.

Less challenging for pot growing would be the dwarf runner bean Hestia. They still require a fair amount of water but not as much as their full size cousins. They can be used to provide a very early crop by growing in an 8 inch (20cm) pot in a frost-free greenhouse or cloche or even indoors. Starting them off in mid-March will give you a very early crop before the main crops come in late July to run through to October.

With all the climbing beans in containers, feed often with good quality tomato feed.

Beetroot

All globe beetroot are suitable for close spacing and container growing. Since beetroot are at their best eaten small (around golf ball size is perfect), rather than leaving them to become woody footballs, sow little and often.

Beetroot seeds are unusual as they are actually a cluster of seeds in one package, so thinning is nearly always required unless pelleted seed is bought, although some varieties come as monogerms, one seed per package. Therefore when you sow you will have to thin out to one seed per station. Beetroot don't really take to transplanting, which means it's best to sow in situ at about 3 inches (8cm) apart each way. However, starting off in modules and transplanting the module can be successful.

All the modern varieties are good. Boltardy, which has the RHS Award of Garden Merit, is a traditional garden favourite since it doesn't run to seed easily like the older varieties. For close growing, try Kestrel which does even better in close spacing for baby beets.

Broccoli and Calabrese

One of the confusions of the broccolis is in the naming. What one seed catalogue (and greengrocer) describes as a broccoli another describes as a calabrese. Whatever the name, most of the broccolis are large plants and not worth trying in small spaces and containers.

The best varieties for close spacing and pot growing in the brassica mix compost are the calabrese types, Kabuki and Sakura being the most successful. Start them off in small pots in April and May, moving on to larger pots as required before planting in the final spot by July for harvesting in October or November.

All the brassicas hate being too cramped in pots as they grow and moving them on to a larger size as the roots hit the bottom of the pot is a good idea.

Even the two Japanese varieties recommended need a fair bit of space though, Kabuki taking the least at a final spacing of 12 inches (30cm) and Sakura needing 18 inches (45cm) minimum. If pot growing, a minimum pot size of 8 inches (20cm) is needed.

Brassicas, being primarily a leaf vegetable, should be fed with a multi-purpose feed high in nitrogen rather than tomato feed.

Brussels Sprouts

I really can't recommend growing sprouts in pots. They need a fair amount of time and space to develop and, unless you have the space for large tubs, they're unlikely to do well.

None is suitable for close spacing, needing between 18 inches (45cm) and 36 inches (90cm) between plants and you can't bring them on too far in pots before planting out. If you really love sprouts, as I do after starting to grow my own, then give them a go but otherwise they're not a good use of limited space.

Cabbage

If you're growing in a small garden's border, then you may be tempted to try the decorative cabbages that have been developed as foliage plants for the flower border. Don't. They just don't have taste. Anyway, I'd contend a proper ball red cabbage is just as attractive as any foliage plant.

There are a number of smaller varieties well suited for both small space growing and container growing. One advantage of these smaller types is that they are the right size for the smaller modern family. The football size cabbage might well make two meals for a family of six or eight but a family of three will be heartily sick of cabbage by the time it is gone.

Minicole is an excellent small cabbage with great flavour, well suited to pot or close spacing. It's also popular with commercial growers for coleslaw making.

Hispi is slightly larger but again has excellent flavour and is suitable for pot and close spacings. Its pointed style looks attractive in mixed pots as well as singly and it matures quickly. It can be grown at most times of the year and would be my choice if I could only grow one variety. It's got the RHS Award of Garden Merit as well.

Pixie is another pointed variety with the RHS Award, although I found Hispi gave me better results.

Puma is a variety that works well for producing 'baby cabbages' at close spacing but if you have enough space to harvest alternately and leave some to grow on, it will produce 1kg (2.2 lb) heads of good quality. It's difficult to find seed though.

Other varieties worth looking at:

Samantha is another well flavoured pointed variety like Hispi and Pixie but not as versatile and Stallion is a compact ball-head for close spacing. April, Candisa and Durham Early are all suitable for close spacing as well.

All the cabbages are best started in modules, moving on to 3 inch (8cm) and then to 5 inch (12cm) pots until space is available for them. Best grown in the brassica mix (see page 51) but they'll generally thrive in most composts so long as they're not acid. I always add a little lime to the compost when growing on and if planting in soil, then a dusting of lime before planting is beneficial.

Feed with a high nitrogen fertilizer to fuel the growth of the leaves. Cabbages are fairly greedy and you will get much better results with regular feeding.

Carrots

If you've ever been to one of the top horticultural shows and seen displays of carrots where the smallest is as tall as a man, then it may surprise you to know they were grown in containers.

The show growers use large barrels, sometimes one on top of another, filled with sand into which they make boreholes and fill these with special composts, often secret mixes that they never reveal lest their rivals find out and steal the coveted red card of the winner at the show along with the £5 prize. Six carrots to the barrel is considered over-crowding by some, so not really in keeping with maximizing crops for small spaces, but great fun anyway.

For table growing you'll be glad to know you don't need to go to these lengths. I actually grow my carrots in bottomless food storage barrels cut into four slices, so about 15 inches (33cm) deep but you can get away with a depth of 8 inches (20cm) or even 6 inches (15cm).

The reason I use cut down barrels, despite having an allotment, is that carrots don't like heavy or stony soil which usually results in those strangely shaped forked carrots and I can control the growing medium by using my carrot compost (see page 51). They'll still do well in ordinary multi-purpose compost though if given a little tomato feed to help them along.

Carrots, a little like potatoes, come in early varieties and main crop varieties. For containers only use the early varieties as these are smaller and faster. I also think they're better flavoured but that's a matter of individual taste.

They hate being transplanted, so sow in situ. There are two methods you can use. For a trough of nothing but carrots, scatter the seeds thinly across the surface and just dust with compost or a little sand to stop them blowing away. Water in and, when the seeds germinate, thin out by just pulling the small seedlings to give them about half an inch (just over 1cm) clear each.

As they grow on, pull out alternate small carrots which are fine to eat, leaving the rest to grow on. A chef friend of mine commented that you'd pay a fortune for those thinnings in his restaurant!

One pest of carrots is the carrot root fly. The fly's maggots cause the damage, killing seedlings and tunnelling just under the skin of more mature plants, leaving brown tunnels behind. The flies produce two generations in a year and are active in April/May and July/August, which almost ensures they can get at our crops.

The fly is attracted by the smell of carrots and is most active in the day so thinning, which bruises foliage and releases the scent, is best carried out late in the day to avoid their notice.

Because the fly tends (notice that, it tends) to fly near the ground, putting up a vertical barrier is often advocated to keep the fly off or planting higher. Unless you're growing on a balcony, I'd suggest covering with horticultural fleece supported above the foliage if the fly is a problem in your area or growing the resistant varieties like Maestro and Flyaway.

One method to defeat the fly, promoted by organic growers in particular, is interplanting with onions as the stronger smell of the onions is supposed to confuse the fly and camouflage the carrot smell. I've not found this interplanting to be 100 per cent successful, but I think it has some effect so this is my second method for container growing carrots. Sow a row of carrots, then a row of spring onions and so forth. The same thinning method as applied above works well.

There are quite a few varieties suitable for container growing. My favourites are the Early Nantes and Amsterdam Forcing types; the Sugarsnax and Tendersnax are excellent as are the fly resistant Maestro and Flyaway mentioned above, but the best variety I've found is Touchon. This is a popular variety in France but harder to find in Britain; it's worth searching out though.

Cauliflowers

Cauliflowers are a crop that can be grown in pots – minimum size 10 inch (25cm) – or a bucket, but they do better with more space in a border or bed. Don't forget when pot growing that the leaves will spread out quite a distance from the pot. There are a number of varieties described as suitable for close spacing but this results in small curds. Conventionally grown cauliflowers will often react to damage, such as caterpillars, or not enough nutrition in the soil by prematurely forming small heads.

If you're really tight for space, I'd give cauliflowers a miss but if you want to try them, then grow like cabbages. The following varieties are described as suitable for close spacing: Avalanche, Igloo, Lateman.

Celeriac

Celeriac is a root crop that has a celery like taste. It's not suitable for close spacing and, while theoretically you could grow one per tub, it's not practical for container growing. Once again, its space requirements make it a poor contender for precious space even if a bed is available.

Celery

Celery is basically a bog plant and requires plenty of rich soil both to provide nutrition and to act as a water reservoir. Show growers will provide 30 gallons of water per plant per week in dry spells! Modern self blanching varieties are planted in blocks about 9 inches (22cm) apart each way and are just not suitable for close spacing. So not a plant I'd grow in containers and I wouldn't grow in a raised bed as it's such poor value for space.

Chilli Peppers
See Peppers, page 90.

Courgettes
Courgettes are incredibly productive croppers and new growers are so often caught out by them, planting half a dozen and wondering what to do when the family refuse to eat courgettes for breakfast as well as every other meal.

Because they're so productive, they need a lot of food and water to give of their best. I'd suggest that growing just one plant in an old bucket or similar will cover most people's needs. Sow initially into 3 inch (8cm) pots indoors in March to May and move to the final site when the last risk of frost has passed. As they crop, feed with tomato feed to keep them going.

It's important to remove the courgettes regularly so that they continue to crop. If you just leave the courgettes to turn into marrows, the plant stops producing more.

Tosca is a superb variety or try Midnight, Venus, Partenon and Supremo, which has the RHS Award of Garden Merit.

One problem courgettes can suffer is powdery mildew towards the end of the season. I rarely worry about it as usually they're not going to last much longer anyway when it strikes and I don't like using fungicides on my food but there is a simple remedy that is safe and does work.

At the first sign of powdery mildew, small white patches on the leaves, spray with a mixture made of 1 part skimmed milk to 4 parts water. Skimmed milk is best as full fat milk can get a little smelly. I've no idea how or why it works, but it does.

Cucumbers

If you've only eaten shop bought cucumber, then you are in for a revelation when you grow your own. Instead of long pretty tasteless tubes of water where half usually ends up in the fridge drying out and mouldering, you will discover a subtle and delicious flavour.

They're an ideal crop for pot growing, in fact I've come to the conclusion that they do better in pots than in the border of a greenhouse or in soil and, because you train the shoots up canes or nets, they're extremely productive from a small area.

Some varieties have been bred for growing in the greenhouse and others for outdoors but even 'outdoors' types will benefit from some protection and a sunny spot, giving you a longer season.

The older varieties had both male and female flowers which meant that you needed to remove the male flowers as soon as they were seen or the fruits would develop a bitter flavour. Modern F1 varieties with female only flowers are far easier, especially for the new grower.

The seeds can be quite expensive, but you only need one plant to provide plenty of cucumbers for a family and cucumber seeds can last seven years if stored correctly, so it's worth paying for the best. Generally sow two seeds, one being a spare, and tuck the rest safely away.

Start them off by sowing one seed per 3 inch (8cm) pot in a multi-purpose compost on a warm window sill. The seeds are flat ovals and should be sown sideways in the pot to stop water sitting on them and causing them to rot off.

When the roots start to push the pot, move on to an 8 inch (20cm) or 10 inch (25cm) pot (or an old bucket) or a grow bag but avoid sudden changes in temperature when you put them outdoors. If the weather is bad and indoor space is limited, move onto an intermediate 5 inch (12.5cm) pot to buy some time. They'll die if they get frosted and they don't like cold nights either. Keep them under a warm cover or bring them indoors for the night until warm evenings arrive.

Cucumbers are susceptible to cucumber mosaic virus, which is passed by aphids, so controlling greenfly is quite important but I've not actually found it a real problem. They can also succumb to powdery mildew towards the end of the season like the courgettes. The dilute milk treatment can gain you a few more productive weeks.

The cucumber is a strange plant. The fruit is 95 per cent water and the plant has a lot of foliage so they need a lot of water but the biggest problem is the stem rotting off where it meets the soil when it is wet.

The answer to this is to sit the pot in a saucer or seed tray without holes so water is held below the pot and then to insert a funnel or half a lemonade bottle top-down into the top and water through that so the surface of the compost is dry. With grow bags, always water through a bottomless pot into the bag rather than around the plant.

Having said that about the stem, they do like a high humidity so mist spray if you can in hot weather. Although they like it warm, too much direct hot sunlight can scorch the plant so provide some shade if we have a glorious summer.

When the leading stem has developed eight leaves, pinch out the growing tip so that side shoots develop bearing extra fruits. Don't forget to keep harvesting as the plant will stop producing if you leave fruits on. Feed as tomatoes when the fruits begin to develop.

The best varieties for small space growing produce small fruits, 4–6 inches (10–15cm) long, but this isn't a problem. Much of the larger cucumbers tend to end up in the bin whereas the smaller ones are perfect for using in one go.

Cucino is an excellent variety if you can provide shelter, as is Picolino, but look for the F1 hybrid all-female flowered version of Picolino. For outdoor growing, Burpless Tasty Green is an excellent flavoured variety but the skin is spiky so it needs peeling before use.

Garlic

You can grow garlic at one per 8 inch (20cm) pot but it's really not worth it. However, if you have some border space, then give garlic a go by all means. Do not just buy a garlic bulb in the supermarket to plant out. It is going to be a foreign variety, bred for warmer climates than ours most likely and the chances of it producing a decent crop in an average year here are slim at best. Buy some stock that has been bred for growing in our climate.

It's remarkably easy. Break the bulb into individual cloves, discarding any very small ones, and drop them into a hole about 4 inches (10cm) deep in November or December about 8 inches (20cm) apart. Leave until June or July when the foliage is yellowing and then dig up the bulbs of garlic.

If you miss sowing in winter, you can sow in early spring but the resultant crop will not be so heavy. Cultivation is simple, just keep the plants from being swamped by weeds and other plants, and water in dry weather.

If you have a heavy clay soil, drop a pinch of sand or fine gravel into the hole before dropping the clove in to stop water-logging causing it to rot.

Allow to dry off for a week or so before storing in a dark, cool and dry place and reserve one or two bulbs to provide next year's stock. You can use garlic immediately as wet garlic in cooking. The taste is much milder than when it has dried.

Kale

A large plant that stands well in the winter so providing a crop when there is little else available fresh. Not suitable for pot growing but possible in a border. Kale needs a lot of room though so it's not good value for space.

Kohlrabi

Kohlrabi is a popular vegetable on the continent yet hardly known in the UK. It's an unusual looking plant, like a beetroot but the leaves grow around and out of the root. It can be eaten cooked or grated/thinly sliced in a salad. The young leaves can also be eaten in salads.

It's best harvested at golf-ball size, which only takes eight weeks from sowing, as larger bulbs become a little woody. It's best sown directly in place, rather than transplanted, and thinned to just 3 inches (8cm) apart. Can be grown in pots or borders and the unusual looks make it ideal for mixed large pots as a decorative item.

Leeks

Leeks can be grown successfully in large pots or troughs. On the normal vegetable plot the seed is sown in a seed bed and then transplanted into holes to grow on for harvesting in winter.

To maximize yield from a small space or a pot we can adjust this system. Sow the seeds thinly in a trough or large pot at least 8 inches (20cm) deep, preferably 1 foot (30cm), in a multi-purpose compost in March or April. Initially feed with slow release fertilizer or liquid feed after six weeks, and then with a general fertilizer mix every 3 weeks after that.

If they're overcrowded, thin out at the seedling stage otherwise leave until the leeks are about pencil thick. These can then either be thinned out to about 3 inch (8cm) spacing or transplanted. The thinnings are rather nice cooked in stir fries rather like spring onions.

If transplanting, dib holes about 6 inches (15cm) deep and just drop the plant into the hole. Water in well but don't push compost into the hole. This will exclude light from the growing point where the leaves meet the white stalk which is also known as 'the blanch' and so you will get a 6 inch (15cm) blanch.

If leaving in place, then make a collar from cardboard – a toilet roll inner is ideal. Cut lengthways, place around the plant and tie on or use an elastic band. To get more blanch, gradually move the collar upwards as the plant grows.

One of the best varieties for home growing for the table is Pancho, which has the RHS Award of Garden Merit. Oarsman is also suitable for close spacing as are King Richard, Edison and Carlton, another RHS Award of Garden Merit winner.

Lettuce and Leaves

If all I had was a window box, then I'd plant some cut and come again leaves. The concept is simple. You scatter the seeds on the compost and just lightly move it around to settle them before watering in.

Fig. 18. Window box lettuce.

When you want some salad leaves, you just cut them off so getting exactly the amount you want. The leaves will re-grow and you can get three or four cuts before they're finally exhausted.

Rather than just one variety, you can buy mixed leaf packs, sometimes themed like 'Italian Salad Mix', or you can make up your own by buying separate packets and mixing the seeds. A typical mix would be: rocket, sweet basil, mizuna, mustard, oak leaf lettuce, radicchio and raab broccoli.

If you prefer a more conventional lettuce, then go for Tom Thumb, Pinokkio and Little Gem. These will provide a handy size for a salad and will do well closely spaced or in a mixed pot.

For an unusual variation on the 'cut and come again' type of salad, if you've got some spare brassica (cabbage family) seeds, sow into a seed tray and snip off at the seedling stage. They're surprisingly tasty as part of a salad.

Spring Onions

Spring onions are a very easy crop to grow and are perfect for pot growing. As an experiment, I've grown spring onions in a seed tray of compost so can confirm they only need a couple of inches' depth of soil.

They don't take much room and are great for tucking into spaces in mixed containers and beds. As a rule, don't provide any special conditions. Just sow thinly and shallowly in situ with the lightest covering of compost above. Try and sow a few every fortnight for a continual supply from March onwards.

I've heard mixing them with carrots is a good idea to confuse the carrot root fly but can't say it's worked for me, although in fairness I may have had a worse problem without them.

Guardsman (RHS Award of Garden Merit), with its vertical pencil stems, is recommended for containers but I've found that the old White Lisbon variety is just as good. You can also get White Lisbon Winter Hardy which is different from just White Lisbon. It is frost resistant and sowings in late summer and autumn will provide a very early spring crop. My favourite is North Holland Blood Red. The reason is that it provides spring onions but, if you have room and just leave it, it will bulb up and provide a small full-size onion.

Onions and Shallots

Ordinary bulb onions and shallots are not worth growing in pots. You'd be looking at one large pot per onion and it doesn't make sense when there are better value crops to grow. If you want to grow onions in a bed, the easiest way is to grow from sets. These are just small bulbs that are planted in the final position to grow on. I doubt ordinary onions are worthwhile when space is short but the over-wintering Japanese types, like shallots, are standing through the winter when there is little competition for space. Still there is a lot of competition for space come the spring. Shallots are not a plant to close space as it just reduces the yield. With onions you can space fairly closely, down to about 4 inches (10cm) apart but this t results in small onions.

Parsnip

The parsnip will do well in large pots or tubs filled with carrot and parsnip compost mix (see page 51) or in beds and borders so long as the soil isn't too heavy. The parsnip has a reputation for being a hard seed to germinate but in large part this is due to people insisting on sowing it in February when the soil is cold and wet. Sowing later, even up to May, will, in my experience, produce perfectly acceptable crops with higher germination rates. The parsnip tastes much better after it has had a frost or two so I see little point in aiming for early crops.

The parsnip doesn't like transplanting at all. Even grown one per module and the module planted tends to result in twisted and forked roots so sow in situ and then thin out as the seedlings develop.

Full sized parsnips need about 6 inches (15cm) or more between plants. Closer spacing results in smaller roots and misshapen roots but there are varieties, such as Lancer, Dagger and Avonresister now available, which are suitable for close spacing.

Peas

Really fresh garden peas are unbeatable. I know you're supposed to cook them but straight from the pod they're delicious raw. The good news is that they're actually an ideal crop for small space and pot growing.

Sow directly in multi-purpose compost and give compact varieties some tomato feed to keep them going when the pods begin to form. For tall varieties, alternate with an ordinary general purpose feed to keep the foliage going.

You sow in March, about half an inch (just over 1cm) deep, and then sow successionally through to June. You can start off in modules and transplant but be aware that the roots grow faster than the foliage will lead you to believe, so don't try to hold for too long. Go for varieties described as early since these crop in the shortest time.

Peas are described as wrinkled or smooth, which refers to the appearance of the seeds. You'll find the wrinkled types sweeter as a rule.

The container variety Half Pint will do well in a reasonable sized pot, 8 inch (20cm) or so, without any support. It grows to about 15 inches (33cm) tall and being bushy is self-supporting. Otherwise any dwarf variety will do.

Better still, if you have some vertical space, is to grow a taller variety up canes or netting, which will give you excellent crop quantity for the space.

The winner of ten RHS gold medals, Medwyn Williams MBE FNVS, grew the variety 'Show Perfection' (which he considers excellent for culinary use) for his stand at Chelsea in 2002 in 7 inch (17.5cm) pots but any tall variety is going to make use of the vertical space and produce a lot of crop in a small area.

For home growing, use deep troughs with canes and netting to support the peas.

Don't forget they'll need a fair amount of water, especially when mature with a lot of foliage.

Peppers

Both sweet peppers and chilli peppers do well in pots. In fact, I think they do better in a pot than in a greenhouse border generally. The trick with peppers is to give them a long growing season and keep them warm. They can be grown without cover in a good year but providing a cloche or at least a sheltered, sunny spot will increase your success.

Start off in late February to the first half of March for sweet peppers and slightly later for hot chilli peppers in a propagator or on a warm window sill. Move on to a 3 inch (8cm) pot when the seedling is large enough to handle and once the roots start to push the base of the pot, or it is about 4 inches (10cm) high, move on to an 8 inch (20cm) pot of multi-purpose compost or a grow bag with a pot inserted.

You'll find that the weight of large sweet peppers or a large number of small hot peppers can break the stems as they grow, so tie onto some canes inserted into the pot to support them.

Fig. 19. Chilli peppers in a pot.

When the flowers open, a mist spray of water will help the fruit set. Feed as tomatoes when the peppers start to develop. With sweet peppers, there is little change in flavour as they change colour but red and yellow peppers do brighten up a salad.

With chilli peppers there's a trend to growing the hottest pepper. Macho growing! The fact is that most chilli peppers are hot enough and going for the incredibly hot varieties can result in effectively unusable crops.

The 'hotness' of the chilli pepper is caused by a chemical called capsaicin and the more of this, the hotter the chilli. The measure of this hotness is made in Scoville units, named after the test's inventor. The hottest pepper ever tested was the Naga Jolokia, an Indian pepper at 1,040,000 Scovilles but the record is now held by Bhut Jolokia according to the *Guinness Book of Records*. The Habanero chillies run around the 100,000 to 350,000 level and the Jalapeno at 2,500–8,000. A

Jalapeno is, in my opinion as a hot curry fan, as hot as anyone could sensibly want to grow but it's up to you.

Incidentally, a glut of chilli peppers is not a problem. Just use some thin wire – the sort of wire sold for tying plants is ideal – and string them through the stems. Then hang them up in an airy, warm and dry place. They'll store for a year easily when dried.

Smaller varieties especially suitable for pots:

Redskin (sweet), Gourmet (sweet with RHS Award of Garden merit), Peperone Cuneo Giallo (sweet), Apache (chilli), Bulgarian Carrot (chilli and they do look like carrots), Barancio (sweet), Roberta (sweet), Demon Red (chilli), Habanero (chilli – very hot), Fatalii (chilli –very hot), Cheyenne (chilli – hot), Inferno (chilli – hot), Super Chili (chilli – hot Thai variety), Mini Bell (sweet), Mohawk (sweet), Sweet Ingrid (sweet).

Potatoes

Surprisingly to many, the potato is a crop that does really well in large pots. The show growers wouldn't dream of growing their five perfect matched specimens in soil. They use bags with special peat based compost mixes that have been shredded to avoid any twigs causing a blemish on the skins.

I wouldn't suggest going to quite those lengths but it is well worth growing some potatoes on the patio. You do need a large pot or you can buy the black plastic bags the show growers use and plant one seed potato per 14 litre bag. If you have more room, then you can get larger bags or even a patio potato barrel which takes five seed potatoes.

Potatoes are a hungry crop and they need plenty of water but they're very productive. Just use an ordinary multi-purpose compost and either add some specialist potato fertilizer or liquid feed with tomato fertilizer. See page 51.

Potato varieties are split into first early, second early and maincrop. The 'early' refers to the time between planting and getting a crop, not that you should plant them earlier than maincrop. Earlies are ready to start harvesting after 12 weeks

Fig. 20. Potato barrel.

but the maincrops that yield more per tuber take 10 weeks longer and require more space so, for small space and container growing, stick with the first early varieties, which are the quickest.

There are literally hundreds of varieties available to the home grower, so you can grow something you will never find in a shop and with a flavour you won't believe. My favourite variety for pot growing would have to be Swift, but your taste may differ. Swift has an advantage that you can eat it as a small new potato but if left will grow on to a potato of baking size. It's a good all-rounder, making nice roasties and chips as well as good for boiling and mashing.

Traditionally you plant potatoes at Easter but you can get away with early March so long as you keep frost away from the foliage. Potatoes are a member of the tomato family and like tomatoes cannot tolerate frost. If there is a cold snap, cover with horticultural fleece or even crumpled newspaper to keep the frost off the foliage.

The biggest problem affecting potatoes is the potato blight. This starts as small patches on the leaves but in as little as 24 hours can spread all over and effectively kill the plant.

However, blight depends on the weather being both warm and humid which tends to come later in the season, after the first earlies have cropped, so it's not a problem you should need to be concerned with.

If you grow in one of the purpose made potato barrels with opening doors at the bottom, you can harvest enough for a meal and close the door, leaving the small developing tubers to grow on. With bag growing, you have to harvest a plant at a time. Keep potatoes in the dark because light will cause them to go green and green potatoes can give you an upset stomach as they contain a mild alkaloid poison.

Pumpkin and Squash

Sadly both pumpkins and squashes take up a lot of space and aren't a good prospect for small space growing, almost impossible in any reasonably sized pot.

Radish

There really can't be an easier crop for pot growing than the salad radish. If you've got a spare square inch, just drop a couple of radish seeds in and thin to one if both germinate. They're great for filling vacant space and they're really quick. From sowing to eating size is just around three weeks.

Not a fussy crop, the radish will grow well in most soil types. Don't leave them too long though as they quickly turn woody; harvest when they reach a reasonable size. Just sow a few each week from March through September for a continual supply throughout the season.

There are winter radishes, the Chinese or mooli types, but these are much larger than the salad radish; more like parsnips. I don't think they're really worth container growing but theoretically there's no reason why not.

Romanesco
Romanesco is a sort of cross between broccoli and cauliflower which appears in either or both sections of the seed catalogues according to how the seedsman feels as far as I can tell. Fine flavoured and nutritious but a large plant with a long growing season so like Brussels sprouts it's not one for the small space grower.

Salsify and Scorzonera
These are root crops similar to parsnips but not from the same family. They're very rarely seen in the shops because they are not well known and so are not popular but their flavour is considered far superior to parsnips. Salsify is often referred to as the vegetable oyster due to its subtle flavour. Scorzonera is similar in flavour but has a black skinned root.

They require a good depth of light soil and are well suited to growing in deep raised beds and large containers like parsnips.

Sow three seeds per position direct in late April, early May at 6 inch (15cm) spacing, ½ inch (just over 1cm) deep, thinning out to the best seedling and harvest from mid-October. Unlike parsnips, they don't store well and culinary preparation is a little more difficult; scalding will make the skin easier to scrape off and then steam or boil until tender.

Spinach and Perpetual Spinach
True spinach is a tricky crop, very prone to bolting (going to seed) that I wouldn't try to grow in pots except for some varieties like Bordeaux, Fiorana, Galaxy or Koto that can be grown as baby salad leaves. In a bed or border, unusually for a vegetable, spinach actually benefits from some shade as too much sun encourages bolting.

Start in modules, successively sowing every two weeks in April and May and then plant out about a foot (30cm) apart. Since you'll be thinning to one seedling per module, use those thinnings raw in a salad.

Pick from the outside of the plant, allowing the centre

leaves to grow on. Spinach reduces a lot when cooked, so you need more than you may expect for a decent meal.

Perpetual spinach, also known as beet leaf, Swiss chard or ruby chard (confusing isn't it?), can be profitably grown in pots. Since some, such as Bright Lights (RHS Award of Garden Merit winner), are stunning looking, they will grace any flower border.

Sow directly in 8 inch (20cm) pots or tubs as the centre-piece of a display in late April to early June and then just harvest the stalks as required. Don't empty the pot at the end of the year. Left throughout the winter the plant will burst back into life for a very early spring crop for you.

Swede

Swedes are not suitable for close spacing and not worth trying to grow in pots; one per 8 inch (20cm) pot is hardly good value. You could grow in a bed or border but they are not recommended for small space growing.

Sweetcorn

Straight from the plant, really fresh sweetcorn is one of the best tasting vegetables you can grow but sadly it isn't suitable for pots or close spacing. It's a very hungry plant, demanding a lot of nitrogen to fuel the growth of the 6 feet (183cm) high stems and foliage. The size of which is the first problem. For the best results you need 18 inches (45cm) distance each way per plant and the heavy shade doesn't make underplanting viable. Even the mini or baby sweetcorns like Minipop grow on large stems, so we're no better off with them.

The next problem with sweetcorn is the way they fertilize. The male flower is at the top of the stem and the pollen falls onto the female flowers on the cob below. If unfertilized, the cobs develop without the corn itself. Because of this to ensure germination they're normally sown in a block.

You could try growing a row in a border at the back but you'd need to manually transfer pollen from the male flowers to the female tassels to reliably get actual corn on the cobs if you only had a couple of lonely plants.

So because of the size and fertilization of the corn, I'd suggest you give sweetcorn a miss.

Tomatoes

Tomatoes are a great crop for the gardener limited in space. Even just a pot on a balcony or a single hanging basket will provide a significant amount from next to no space at all. Because they are so valuable and popular a crop, I think it is worth addressing growing tomatoes in detail.

In addition to the fact that the taste of any sun-warm tomato straight from the plant is far superior to anything you can buy from a shop, you can get literally hundreds of different varieties and grow the tomatoes with exactly the flavour you and your family prefer.

Apart from fruit size, flavour and colour, tomatoes come in three main types. The first and most common is the tall indeterminate or cordon types. With these, the side shoots will grow out, sub-dividing and producing a giant bush if not stopped by pinching out. This type is ideal for growing up a cane or string from a pot or grow bag.

The bush or determinate type of tomato, where the side branches develop naturally forming a bush that stops itself eventually, are generally too large for container or small space growing.

Dwarf varieties are very small bush types, often grown in hanging baskets or small containers.

Although you can buy plants and even propagate more plants from the plants as I explained in Seeds and Plants, page 56, by growing from seed you will have access to a far wider choice.

Tomato seeds will store for three years but, if you want to grow one or two plants from a number of varieties, you could swap seed with a friend or even start a number off in small pots and sell them from the door. At 50p per plant there's a tidy profit to be made!

Some varieties are more suited to greenhouse growing and

some to outdoor growing although they benefit from a sheltered sunny spot. So spend some time carefully researching before you buy seeds depending on your situation.

All tomatoes are started off in heat. You can use either a propagator or warm window sill. Sow the seeds in a small shallow pot. When large enough to handle, move them into a 3 inch (8cm) pot. Start varieties for the greenhouse earlier than those for outdoors: usually early March is OK for the former, and the second half of March for the latter.

By the beginning of May, they will be ready for planting on into their final home. As they do not grow well below 10°C, if May is cold it is helpful to provide some night heating. Tomatoes cannot tolerate even a mild frost.

The quantity and quality of the crop depends on how well the plant is developed and its ability to convert nutrients into fruit. This, in turn, depends on the roots. A better root development produces a better plant.

If you look closely at the base of the stem, you will see thin hairs growing. These 'hairs' turn into roots if they are in the soil, so plant deeply when you move from one pot size to the next and you will produce more roots to boost growth quickly.

Growing in Grow Bags

Producers of grow bags usually advise planting three tomatoes per bag but this really does not provide enough compost. Take two 8 inch (20cm) or larger pots and cut the base off them. Fit into the grow bag so the bag forms the base and then fill the pots with the contents of another grow bag or just some multi-purpose compost. Plant deeply into those pots and the roots will have more room to develop and the compost is less likely to dry out if you forget to water.

With the grow bag in position, pierce some holes just over 1 inch (3cm) above the floor level. These will drain excess water if you over-water at any time. Next, insert a small pot between the large pots. You can water into this as well as into the large pots.

Whichever method you use to plant, you need to insert a bamboo cane by the stem. As the tomato grows, tie it to the cane to keep it supported.

Fig. 21. Growing tomatoes in a grow bag.

Tomatoes must be watered regularly. In hot, sunny weather they may well need double the amount of water required on a cloudy day, so make sure that you have watered thoroughly and not just wet the surface of the compost. If you water irregularly, the fruits will split and blossom end rot – where the base of the fruit rots – will develop.

As the plant grows, tie in the main stem every 12–18 inches (30–45cm) up the stake and keep nipping out side shoots before they get much over an inch (3cm) long. Side shoots form at the joint between the stem and leaf. We want to encourage the plant to put its energy into fruit, not into growing masses of foliage.

To help the fruit in dry weather, use mist spraying. Apart from that, you only need to feed the plant. Once the fruit begin to swell, use a commercial tomato fertilizer as per the instructions. Be careful not to over feed. It will not benefit you and can actually cause problems.

When the plant has reached the top of the cane or seven trusses of fruit (if growing in a greenhouse), or four or five trusses (if growing outdoors), have begun to form, pinch out the growing tip about two leaves above the last truss. A truss is the stem on which the tomatoes grow.

This will force the plant to put all its energy into the crop which will be ready before the season ends. The plant will react to this by trying to grow even more side shoots, so you need to inspect daily when watering and pinch out.

Towards the end of the season, remove any leaves shading fruits to help them ripen. Tomatoes are susceptible to tobacco mosaic virus so if you are a smoker, don't smoke around your plants and wash your hands before handling them.

With outdoors plants, the further you bring them on in shelter, the better before hardening off.

The tumbler types do well in hanging baskets and jardinières; they can look very decorative when under-planted with trailing lobelia or even marigolds to deter whitefly.

The chances are you will have some green tomatoes left on the plant at the end of the season. These can be used in chutney or ripened by putting into a bowl with some ripe bananas. The bananas release minute amounts of ethylene gas that promotes many fruits to ripen.

Feeding with cheap commercial tomato feeds and overfeeding can cause locking out of magnesium which is needed to enable the plant to take up nitrogen. In effect a vitamin deficiency, the symptom being yellowing between the veins on the leaves starting lower down on the plant and moving up if unchecked.

Treatment is really easy. Buy some Epsom salts from the chemist and mix 30g per litre of warm water. Allow to cool and spray the plants each couple of days, adding about 10g per plant into the water when watering.

Sometimes you will find that the leaves have curled up on the plants, this is actually nothing to worry about and tends to happen as the nights get cooler.

Turnip

Turnips are ideal for container growing, particularly the varieties that are best harvested at ping-pong ball size. Atlantic and Tokyo Cross (RHS Award of Garden Merit) are especially recommended for growing in pots, having been bred for eating at a young stage.

Sow directly and thin to just an inch and a half (4cm) apart from the end of April through July for a continual supply at the peak of perfection.

8

FRUIT

You might be surprised by the range of fruits and types of fruit you can grow in a limited space or containers. Having seen cherry trees so tall you can't see the cherries at the top or overgrown old apple trees where you would get vertigo trying to climb them, you may well have written fruit off for small space growing except for strawberries, of course.

The breeder's art has changed all that. Tree fruits like apples and cherries are actually two part trees. The fruiting stem, technically called a scion, is the variety but that is grafted onto a rootstock. The reason they're grown this way is that the rootstock is what decides how large and vigorous the final tree will be. Trees that grow too large, or require a lot of pruning to keep to a reasonable size, are inefficient for the commercial growers, so the industry came up with dwarfing rootstocks.

While varieties of apples have evocative names like Barnack Beauty or Chiver's Delight, rootstocks for apples are referred to by letters and numbers The letters stand for the trial ground, either Malling or Malling Merton, and the number comes from the trial number. There is no relationship between the number and size: M27 produces a smaller tree than M9 or M7, for example. Most varieties of apple, pear, cherry or plum can be grown in a pot, so long as the correct rootstock is used.

A decent nursery will not only be able to tell you what the rootstock is but also what rootstock and variety is likely to do well for your soil conditions and locality. It's well worth paying a little extra for the expertise and advice of a specialist as your fruit tree will be there for many years to come.

My experience with bargain fruit bushes from chain stores has been that they disappoint in the end. Even when they're a named variety, they haven't done well. After two or three years you won't remember what you have paid but you will be regretting that bargain offer.

All bushes and fruit trees are a long-term investment, often taking a couple of years before you start to see a return. If you find yourself moving house, like many of us have to for work, don't forget that the pot grown tree can move with you.

With tree fruit you might wonder, 'Why don't I grow it from a pip or stone?' There is a good reason. The pip or stone will be a cross between the variety you've eaten and another unknown variety. If it is viable it will be years before you even know if it will produce an edible fruit. The chances of a decent fruit are remarkably slim, less than 1 per cent.

Most bush fruits will do well in containers, although they do need to be a reasonable size and even in a large garden some fruits like the blueberry are easiest to grow in containers. One use for an old bath is to grow blueberries or cranberries. They like a boggy soil so the plughole provides enough drainage to prevent waterlog developing and the bath is large enough for three bushes.

As with vegetables, it's not sensible to grow all fruits in containers or small spaces so I've concentrated on the ones that are worthwhile for a small garden or for tub growing. With fruit trees and bushes, unless I state otherwise, use a John Innes compost but add some water retaining gel crystals since trees and bushes use more water than you expect and drying out, especially when the fruit is forming, is not good for them.

With the tree fruit, feed each spring with a slow release general fertilizer or give a monthly liquid feed. In the late winter give an additional feed high in potash (sulphate of potash) and some bonemeal as a slow release of and calcium (especially for stone fruits) to ensure a good crop.

Fig. 22. Minarette apple tree in a pot.

Apples

For container growing I would recommend the minarette style, which will also do well in small beds and borders, only needing to be spaced 2–3 feet (0.5–1 metre) apart. Minarettes are slender, with the fruit bearing on short spurs directly off the vertical main stem rather than from branches. They grow to 6–8 feet (about 2 metres) tall but do not spread so they really make good use of space.

Even better use of space can be had with a duo-minarette. These have two varieties growing one above the other on the same stem. (They are available from Ken Muir Nurseries among others.) The minarettes are extremely productive, with sometimes as many as 50 apples from one plant, so you're not just growing a token tree. They're also very easy and quick to prune, so saving your time.

You are not limited to a minarette tree in a container. Apples can be pruned into a remarkable number of shapes and a pyramid style can look very good in a tub. M26 is considered the best rootstock for container growing.

One other benefit of container growing with apples is that the constriction of the roots tends to push them into fruiting earlier than larger trees that may not start production for a few years.

Once your tree has moved into its final pot or tub, you can underplant with any shallow rooting plants to maximize production. Don't be too eager to pot on though, or you'll delay fruit production.

A possible difficulty with apples in a small garden is that many varieties require an apple of a different variety to pollinate them in order to produce fruit. It can't be just any variety either; it has to be one that flowers around the same time. Some are self-fertile but will do better with a separate variety pollinating. If you already have a crab apple, that may well be able to fill the gap and it's worth peering over the fence to check what the neighbours have as their crab apple could act as a pollinator for you. Once again, check with your supplier.

One answer to the multiple varieties problem is to grow a family tree. Generally three scions are grafted onto the single rootstock thereby providing three different types of apple from the one tree. They're not suitable for containers but if you have room for a tree in the garden that will eventually grow to about 10–12 feet (3.5 metres) high and spread a similar distance, these family trees are well worth considering.

Growing along a fence offers possibilities for apples. First, there is the cordon where the stem is grown at an angle, usually near 45 degrees, with short fruiting spurs. The beauty of these is that the trees can be spaced at 2 feet (0.5 metre) apart, enabling different varieties to be planted in a small space. The trees are tied to wires and pruned each spring.

Avoid tip bearing varieties as you'll be cutting off the fruiting tips each spring. The best rootstocks to use are M9, M26 and MM106.

Another option for growing against a fence or wall is an espalier or fan design. Here you are getting a tree 'flattened' to the fence, saving space again. Once again M26 and

MM106 rootstocks are suitable but M9 is a little too weak for this.

The last, but not least, option for a small garden is to grow a stepover. Here the tree is trained to a wire about 18–24 inches (45–60cm) above the ground, taking the leader one way and a side branch the other. Stepovers provide a semi-formal edging to a border that's productive as well.

Pears

From a growing point of view, pears are similar to apples except that they flower earlier, which can be a problem in more northerly areas. A cold late frost or northerly wind can strip the blossom so preventing the fruit from developing.

Growing in sheltered spots will alleviate the problem and with cordons or espalier trees choosing a southerly facing fence or, better still, warm wall will help no end.

When buying a pear tree, you will notice that there is not as wide a range of rootstocks. The two you will generally find are Quince A, which is the most common, and the slightly less vigorous Quince C, which is better for cordons. The main thing to ask the nursery about is the flowering time. If you live in a cold spot or in the north and cannot provide shelter, then go for later flowering types like Beurre Hardy or the new self-fertile Concorde.

Like apples you can get minarettes and even the duo minarettes from some nurseries as well as family trees for the garden.

Pears never actually ripen on the tree. They're designed to fall off and then ripen. Bringing them into the house will allow them to ripen but do be careful, once they've hit the peak of perfection they go over very quickly. If you have a glut of pears, they will store for a few weeks in a fridge being brought out for a couple of days ripening in the warm when you're ready.

Cherry

If you only have room for one fruit tree, then it has to be a cherry in my book. But this gives you a dilemma, should it be a sweet eating cherry or an acid cooking cherry? There must be something you can get rid of to get both in!

The biggest pest for the cherry has to be the birds. You see the small green cherries form and then they start to colour up so you go out the next morning feeling hopeful only to find the bare stones hanging on the stalks! Wherever you grow them, to actually get a crop you will need to net the tree.

They not only produce one of our best fruits, they're attractive as plants. The spring blossom brightens the garden when not much else is in flower and the russet autumn leaves last well, adding colour to the depressing end of the year.

Not so long ago, cherries were very difficult for the home grower. They're naturally a very large tree and the only common dwarfing rootstock was Colt, which still resulted in trees a little too large for the average garden let alone a small modern garden. Happily we now have new dwarfing rootstocks like Gisela 5 and Tabel, with more in trial. These mean that we can now even grow our cherries in tubs, which was just impossible 30 years ago.

The other problem that we used to have was a lack of self-fertile varieties. Cherries used to be more than a bit complicated because not only did they need another variety that flowered at the same time nearby, it had to be a compatible variety.

One of the first self-fertile sweet cherries, Stella, revolutionized home cherry growing and now we have quite a range of self-fertile dessert cherries so there really isn't a problem. Do check you are buying self-fertile though. It's easy to misread self-infertile as self-fertile in a catalogue.

All the dessert cherries like full sun but for shady spots you can grow the acid cooking cherries. The self-fertile morello is the most common and in my opinion yet to be beaten, making wonderful jams and pies. Because the acid cherries are naturally less vigorous than the dessert, colt is currently the favoured rootstock producing a tree about 6 feet (just under 2 metres) high.

Cherries are often grown fan-trained against a wall or fence, the desserts on a sunny wall and the acid morello on a north-facing wall in the shade. I cannot think of a more

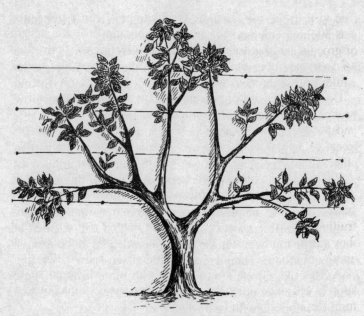

Fig. 23. Fan-trained cherry tree.

productive way to use a north-facing wall than growing cherries. Because they're on a wall or fence, it should be fairly easy to construct a frame to support bird netting.

Young cherries are difficult to prune to shape, although it obviously can be done. If you are looking to grow a fan trained tree it is best to buy one where the nursery has initially shaped it for you. Pruning with cherries is best carried out in the late summer, immediately after fruiting as they're quite susceptible to disease and the pruning wound will heal faster than in the winter.

Plums, Damsons and Gages

This is the last of the native fruit trees I'd recommend for small space growing. When I started gardening the idea of growing any of the plum family in a small garden was laughable and to suggest pot growing a plum tree would get you a free visit to the psychiatrist. The average Victoria plum tree was 30 feet (9 metres) tall, producing enough crop for a chain of grocers, and fan trained specimens were grown against the 16 foot (nearly 5 metre) walls that surrounded the walled gardens of the great estates.

Once again the development of dwarfing rootstocks brought forward a revolution in home growing with the Pixy and St Julienne A rootstocks which make small fan trained trees, dwarf pyramids and even minarette plum trees available.

Plums have a reputation for irregular fruiting, which is down to two things. First, the early flowering varieties are susceptible to frosts destroying the blossom and so preventing fruiting. Second, when they do fruit they're so prolific that they exhaust the tree and the next year they just don't have the energy to produce fruit.

As with the sweet cherries, position in a sheltered sunny spot or provide some protection against frost with horticultural fleece, etc, when flowering.

When the fruit begins to form, usually mid-May, thin the fruit out by removing any that look damaged or diseased and allowing enough space for them to grow to full size without touching a neighbour. It's worth checking again after a month as the fruit will have developed and you'll easily pick out any overcrowding.

One further problem with plums is that if you don't thin, the weight of a lot of fruit can cause branches to break and disease like silver leaf to get in. Because of this susceptibility to silver leaf, pruning is best carried out in early summer.

Be aware plums attract wasps like no other fruit. Hanging some wasp traps around in late June will help somewhat by catching the scouting wasps before they can get back to the nest for reinforcements.

You can build your own wasp trap by taking a jam jar and half filling with sugar water and smearing a little jam just above the waterline. Replace the lid and punch a hole about an inch (2.5cm) wide so forming a bit of a funnel. The wasps go in but find it hard to get back out and so drown.

Types of Plums

Plums come in a range of varieties, some better for cooking and some for eating. There are some sub-varieties of plums as well:

Bullaces – very much a cooking plum, too tart for eating fresh

Gages – sweet dessert plums that are eaten fresh

Damsons – usually somewhat smaller than plums with tart skins, generally eaten cooked but some varieties like Merryweather are good all-rounders and can be eaten fresh

Mirabelles or **Cherry Plums** – these are very hardy, so worth considering if providing a warm spot or protection is difficult.

Some varieties are self-fertile, which simplifies growing tremendously, but some will require a partner to pollinate them. Make sure you know before you buy as finding out you need a partner some five years down the line when you've had no fruit is frustrating!

For a single plum, consider Blue Tit as it is well flavoured, prolific, hardy and has the RHS Award of Garden Merit. It is available as a minarette.

If you fancy two varieties but only have room for one, you can get duo-minarettes now with two types on the same stem.

Plums don't last long. You can keep them for a few days and possibly a day or two longer by keeping in a fridge but they're very much an eat them or lose them crop. When you're faced with a glut you can, of course, bottle or make jams but for a plum pie we find just bagging up and freezing can spread the season for a couple of months.

Figs

Figs to me always conjure visions of an oasis in the dessert, a huge moon in a starlit sky, eating figs in the tent and drinking tiny cups of strong sweet coffee. Back to reality! You can grow figs anywhere in the UK, even in the north of Scotland with the hardy variety Violetta that will tolerate temperatures down to –20°C. The most popular variety for the UK is Brown Turkey which is very reliable and reasonably hardy but Brunswick is said to have a better flavour. Despite the tree itself being hardy, the tips of the branches where the fruit is formed can be damaged by a frost and protecting with fleece, etc, is required to safeguard the fruit.

As the fruit matures, protect with netting or you'll find the birds have harvested them for you.

The fruit is produced by the fig as its method of reproduction and if treated really well the plant sees no need to reproduce and will not fruit. So when growing in a border, you need to restrict the root growth by walling in a 2 foot (60cm) cube with slabs, etc. Even if you have a border, for this reason, I'd suggest container growing anyway.

Its natural condition is to grow in poor soil so a basic John Innes compost with grit added at 1 part grit to 4 parts compost by volume will duplicate that. Provide some slow release general fertilizer at about half the normal rate and liquid feed with a tomato fertilizer monthly during the summer but, if the tree seems very vigorous and produces a lot of lush foliage, cut back on the feeding. We want fruit not leaves.

Prune, but not too hard, in the spring and pinch out new growth at five or six leaves in the summer. The fruit should be ready for harvest in late summer and, after fruiting, the fig will often produce another flush of fruit. If these survive the winter, then an early crop can be had. In its natural Mediterranean home it can produce three crops a year but we usually get one.

Citrus Fruit

Lemons, limes and oranges have become quite popular in the UK in recent years but you really need a greenhouse or conservatory to over-winter them so growing in containers is the usual method.

It is critical that you can provide the right conditions in the winter or, quite simply, your tree will die. Some varieties are slightly hardier than others and will tolerate down to 5°C but as a rule, work on 10°C to be safe.

Fig. 24. Lemon tree in a pot.

They can go outside for the summer, but be careful not to move them out until the nights are above 10°C and there is absolutely no danger of frost. This moving of quite large and heavy tubs needs to be considered, especially if you're not fully able. We found a sack truck helpful for moving around our large pot containing a 5 foot (1.5 metre) tree. You can buy these reasonably cheaply from DIY stores.

With citrus, use a similar compost to figs but feed well with a high nitrogen fertilizer in the summer and a balanced fertilizer in spring and autumn as they're quite greedy plants.

Pruning should be carried out in the short dormant period in late winter. When you buy your citrus tree, look for a good structure and check that the joint between the scion and rootstock is good and firm. All the citrus are self-fertile.

SOFT FRUIT

Blackberries and Hybrid Berries

I love blackberries and some of the hybrid berries like the loganberry but sadly most varieties are not suitable for small space growing and none for container growing. The only way realistically to grow them in a small garden is along a fence but you'll need a minimum of 12 feet (3.5 metres) of fence to grow against for most and you could grow a lot of other plants in that space. There are a couple of candidates among the blackberries you could try though: Loch Ness, which is said to need only a 6 foot (1.8 metre) run and Oregon Thornless which needs 8 feet (about 2.5 metres).

If you happen to have a garden backing onto some wasteland, then a few root cuttings from some wild blackberries might just plant themselves on the outside of your fence. In short order they'll be overhanging the fence and providing a free crop as well as improved security. No cultivation required at all!

The easiest method is to buy container grown plants. String wires using vine eyes from the fence post at about 1 foot (30cm) apart, starting at 3 feet (just under a metre) above the ground and then dig a hole about 6 inches (15cm) wider and deeper than the container. Put a handful of bonemeal into the base and mix it into the soil with a fork.

Use a multi-purpose compost mixed 50:50 with soil to bring up to the same height as it was in the container and around the sides. Firm in well. When planted, firm well and water well, then shorten the shoots down to about 9 inches (22cm). The fruit develops on one year old canes and the easiest method is to allow these to grow to one side. The next year's growth is trained up the other side and, after fruiting, the first side is cut off at ground level. Next year the new canes grow up that side so the fruiting side alternates year on year.

There are various other methods of training the canes but they are harder to persevere with and my experience is that you can end up with tangled masses far too easily so that is the one I stick with.

Raspberries

It is possible, just, to grow raspberries in containers but you'll need something at least 2 feet (60cm) square and about 18 inches (45cm) deep to succeed. They're really a border crop if grown in a small garden but unless you really love raspberries I'd give them a miss when space is tight.

Raspberries hate heavy soils and waterlogging, their ideal soil is sandy yet humus rich. If you have heavy clay, you'll need to dig out a trench and put a layer of gravel in to give drainage and then fill with a compost sand mixture. Rake a couple of ounces (60g) per square yard (metre) of general purpose fertilizer into the soil before planting out container grown plants at a minimum of 16 inches (40cm) apart. Although they don't like being waterlogged, they do need quite a lot of water in the summer when growing and producing fruit so water well in dry spells.

Cultivation is not difficult. Just keep them weed free, taking care not to damage the shallow roots, and provide some general purpose fertilizer with a little extra potash in the spring.

Raspberries come in two types (as well as a range of colours from yellow to deep red): summer fruiting and late autumn fruiting varieties. The autumn varieties bear fruit on this year's canes but summer fruits develop on last year's canes. The summer fruiting varieties are more than twice as productive but you'll still need a 6 foot (1.8 metre) run to get 8 lb (3.5kg) of fruit.

With the summer varieties, cut canes that have fruited down to ground level after harvest and tie in the new shoots to wires. The autumn varieties are simpler: in February cut everything down to ground level and tie in the new shoots as they grow.

With both types, just cut off the growing tip when they are as high as you want, usually around 5 feet (1.5 metres).

Strawberries

Now we're onto a fruit that is a must for the smallest space. There is nothing to beat a strawberry straight from the plant, although jam made from your summer crop in the winter comes a close second.

You can, obviously, grow strawberries in a border but by growing in containers you will get a far higher yield per square foot with less time spent cultivating them. Pests are less of a problem with container growing as well. The two main pests, apart from visiting children, are the birds picking off from above and the slugs attacking from below.

Netting will keep the birds away easily enough but the slugs and snails can be a real problem. You may feel safe growing in a hanging basket but it's amazing how tenacious snails can be. Just a half a dozen of the safe slug pellets in a hanging basket will protect the crop.

Almost any pot or container will serve for growing strawberries and mixing with flowers in a hanging basket provides unusual and productive decoration. The hanging plastic flower bags with a number of pockets in a tower work well with strawberries interspersed or just strawberries on their own.

However, the most effective way to grow is in a strawberry barrel with planting cups let into the sides. We have a Victorian style barrel that's actually made of plastic but looks

Fig. 25. Strawberries growing in a hanging basket.

attractive all the same and you don't really notice it in the growing season as the foliage and fruit covers it.

Avoid small pottery and terracotta planters. In my experience, they don't hold enough compost so, even with feeding, the plants don't do so well. They're also prone to drying out in warm spells as there is little reserve to hold water either.

You can buy strawberry seed but usually you would buy plants which are faster to produce fruit and less troublesome – except for alpine strawberries which are grown from seed but only last one season. Don't worry too much about the cost of plants as you'll be propagating your own after buying your original stock.

After three years strawberry plants begin to lose steam so it's time to replace them. Luckily this is easy to do as they naturally grow shoots that have small plants along their length called runners. In the first year after planting, remove all runners as soon as you notice them to keep the plant's energy being used to establish it and provide fruit. From your second and third year plants, you can allow a runner or two per plant to develop and using a piece of wire – coat hanger wire is ideal – bent into a 'V', clip the plantlet on the runner down into a small pot of compost. Cut the runner before the next plantlet and cut away from the mother plant once the plantlet has rooted.

Buy your first plants and plant out ones you have grown yourself in March or April.

Planting up a strawberry barrel is a little strange, especially for experienced gardeners, as you will be planting horizontally. Fill the barrel with compost up to the base of the first planting holes and then feed your plants through the hole, leaf end first, so that the roots lie on top of the compost. Spread the roots out and then add more compost up to the next planting holes. Repeat until you reach the top and then water thoroughly. If your compost is fairly dry when planting up, water each layer as you go to ensure the compost is evenly wetted throughout.

Growing strawberries in deep barrels poking out of the side, or in pouches, creates a problem in getting the water to the roots but not allowing water to pool and stagnate which will drown the plants. Accordingly use a mix of 2 parts good quality multi-purpose compost to 1 part vermiculite by volume adding slow-release fertilizer granules as per the instructions on the pack to establish the plants.

Thereafter feed monthly with tomato feed and, when you come to replace the plants after three years, replace the compost at the same time.

At the end of the year, the leaves will yellow and die back. Take a pair of sharp scissors and just cut them off. This annual haircut ensures no pests are sheltering and clears the decks for next year's growth.

There's quite a range of strawberries available to buy. Summer fruiting varieties produce their fruit over a period of two or three weeks and these are available as early, mid-season and late-season according to when in the summer they fruit. Perpetual strawberries produce small flushes of fruit over the whole season but overall they produce less than the summer varieties.

The easiest variety to find is the commercial mid-season Elsanta. It has good yields, excellent flavour and is reliable. If you can find it, you could try Pegasus instead, which is just as productive but easier for organic growers as it's resistant to botrytis. For jam making, try the mid-season Tenira.

Honeoye is considered the best for an early strawberry, and Florence or Symphony for late-season cropping. For a perpetual, try Flamenco or Mara des Bois.

By growing a range of summer fruiting and perpetual strawberries, you can enjoy them fresh through most of the season but you do need to keep track of which plant is which. They all look pretty much the same so you need to be diligent with labelling when propagating.

Blueberries and Bilberries

A fond memory of my childhood is my grandmother's bilberry pie. Small dark berries full of tart flavour swimming in a thin juice the colour of Quink ink enclosed in a thin melting but rich pastry. Sadly the secret of the pastry passed with her but the blueberries remain.

Blueberries have a high level of anti-oxidants and are claimed to do everything from improve night vision to slow the ageing process and improve memory loss. Never mind all that, they're delicious and not so easy to find in the shops except in cans.

Bilberries can be found growing wild in boggy acid soils in Britain and you can obtain plants to grow but the more culti- vated blueberry is better value for space. Incidentally, the autumn leaf colours of blueberries are spectacular and they really brighten up a patio at a rather sad time of year.

Because the natural conditions are acid wet soils and we need to duplicate these, pot growing is the easiest way. For border growing, we actually sink pots into the border or build a special bed especially for the bog berries.

Although we want a moist-to-wet soil, we don't want them sitting in stagnant water so some care is needed with drainage and the pot itself. Growing in an unglazed terracotta type of pot will allow water to seep through the sides and evaporate. To counter this, line the pot with polythene with holes punched through the base to allow some drainage.

Better still, use glazed pottery or plastic. The ideal containers are the plastic pots where a water well is incorpo- rated in the base. For a large container in a border, consider an old bath sunk into the ground or even standing proud to astound the neighbours. Cover the plug hole with broken pottery shards to stop the compost blocking the hole.

When planted up, mulch the top of the compost with a half inch (1cm) layer of fine gravel. This will stop water evapo- rating from the top and any weeds that take can be spotted and pulled easily.

Being acid loving plants, we need to use an ericaceous compost, which just means it is lime free. A pH of 4.5 to 5.0 is ideal. It's the worst environment for vegetables but the right compost for blueberries, cranberries and other bog berries. Use a John Innes ericaceous compost mixed with a quarter soil-less ericaceous compost by volume and add a generous quantity of water retaining granules.

If you can, water ericaceous plants with rainwater rather

than tap water that can push the pH up. They don't need a lot of feeding, being adapted to a low nutrient environment, but if they are looking a little weak, use half strength ericaceous feed.

After a few years, particularly if using tap water, check the pH level and if it has risen add some sulphur chips to lower it again.

Blueberries are partially self-fertile. If you have just the one plant or two plants of the same variety, they will flower well but the set will be poor and the number of berries low. Ideally two plants of different varieties is the minimum.

Try to buy 2–3 year-old plants, usually in 1.5 or 2 litre pots and move on to 12 inch (30cm) pots as a minimum. Larger pots will do better but you can get away with a 12 inch one for a few years.

In late winter each year, remove one or two of the older stems to encourage new stems to grow. Prune back the new shoots to a couple of buds from the tip and this will encourage the development of side shoots.

Fig. 26. Blueberries underplanted with cranberries.

There's a wide range of varieties available, Bluetta, Herbert and Bluecrop being suitable for smaller containers but Tophat is reputedly the best. You will need to allow space for the spread even if the pot itself is relatively small. Around 2 feet (60cm) all round is about right for a fully grown small blueberry.

Because of the acid soil requirement, underplanting is difficult. Most other crops would just die but you can underplant with cranberries that have a low-growing habit and require the same conditions.

Cranberries

Yet another of the 'superfoods' which are supposed to cure all ills and are probably the active ingredient in the fountain of youth! My scepticism aside, cranberry juice is an excellent diuretic and helpful with urinary tract infections. This American berry was really made famous by Delia Smith's cookery programme and now it is almost compulsory with Christmas dinner.

Cranberries require the same conditions as blueberries so I won't repeat the instructions regarding composts and feeding. Because of their low growing habit – they're naturally a ground cover plant – you can grow them in hanging baskets, window boxes, etc, as well as pots. Do note the instruction in blueberries about keeping the compost moist though. Because they're a ground cover plant, they naturally grow under trees so they'll do well in a shady or semi-shaded spot as well as in full sun.

Once they have fruited, usually in early autumn, give the plants a trim with secateurs or sharp scissors to keep them bushy. They can get quite straggly if left to their own devices.

Lingonberries

I first came across lingonberries in Norway. In times gone by we would always have sweet with meat but now that's limited to apple sauce with pork and possibly redcurrant jelly with lamb. In Scandinavia, however, they still keep to that culinary tradition. We had stopped in a service station and I had meatballs with chips, mushy peas and a big dollop of jam. I was a little hesitant to say the least but the 'jam' was a lingonberry preserve and not only delicious on its own but it went really well with the meatballs.

I asked my Norwegian friend how you grew them and he looked a little puzzled before explaining that you just picked them in the forest where they grow like a weed. Since we don't have many forests, just grow them in exactly the same way as a cranberry, to which they are related.

As you can imagine, being a sub-arctic plant, they're extremely hardy. Minus 40°C won't harm them so don't worry about what our British winter can throw at them.

If you wish to propagate both lingonberries and cranberries, they're quite easy. In autumn when the soil is still warm, remove from the pot or dig up and tease the roots apart, discarding the woody central clump and re-potting sections of the younger root. Water in well and the job is done.

Both cranberries and lingonberries are self-fertile so you don't need to concern yourself with pollinating partners.

Blackcurrants

Blackcurrants are yet another fruit being lauded as a 'super-food' so you can excuse the need for some unhealthy sugar to make the sour fruit palatable. Ninety-five per cent of the black-berries grown commercially in the UK go to drink manufac-turers and I must admit this is one way I like mine. My method is a little different though: fill a jar with blackcurrants and top up with brandy. After six months, mash the blackcurrants in the brandy and strain. A rather nice Christmas liqueur.

A mature bush can produce 10 lb (4.5kg) of currants but they are self-fertile so you only need one bush, unless you want a lot of blackcurrants that is. They're not commonly grown as container plants but some of the more compact varieties will do well in containers. Ben Sarek, Ben Gairn and Ben Connan are the best bets for pots. You will need a large half-barrel size even with compact varieties to do well.

Blackcurrants are greedy plants. Use John Innes No. 3 compost and add a few ounces (60g) of bonemeal along with some general purpose slow-release fertilizer and some water retaining granules.

Normally you look to buy and plant in the winter, from November to March. Plant an inch or two (5cm) deeper than they have been at the nursery, then firm the compost around the plant and cut off all the shoots just above the second bud protruding above ground level. This seems drastic but it encourages root growth and promotes new shoots.

For the first year just feed monthly in the growing season with a general liquid feed and ensure the bush has plenty of water.

In the second winter it is time to start regular pruning. Cut away any damaged shoots and those crossing over each other. Finally remove about a quarter of the old shoots, concentrating on the centre to keep the bush open.

Because of the way they grow and the pruning regime needed to keep them productive, blackcurrants aren't suitable for training into fans and other shapes like the apples, for example.

Do watch out for the birds; netting is advisable. Take the netting down to ground level. I've seen birds learn they can get to the fruit by going in at ground level under the netting and flying up to the feast.

Redcurrants and White Currants

You can grow redcurrants in containers but, unlike blackcurrants, they can be trained as fans and cordons so making growing along the fence a better prospect. For containers use a similar compost mix as for the blackcurrants. If growing in a border, prepare the ground by digging over and adding as much compost as you can plus a good handful of bonemeal mixed into the soil at the bottom of the planting hole.

In the late winter after planting and each year after, give 2–3 oz (70g) of general purpose fertilizer around the plant to fuel the spring growth. With pot grown plants, provide regular liquid feeding each month through the growing season.

Redcurrants are a little strange in that they do far better when pruned. Pruning seems to stimulate them to grow but unpruned they don't get away as fast and seem to stand still for years.

In the first winter after planting you cut the main stems back to about half their length just above an outward facing bud. If you have any shoots below about 4 inches (10cm) high on the main stem, cut these off flush to the stem.

Regular pruning is also carried out in winter when the plant is dormant and the exact method will depend on what final shape you are trying to achieve. Apart from shaping, prune side shoots back to two buds which will force growth to be concentrated and stop the bush from becoming very straggly.

Redcurrants fruit on old wood and at the base of new wood, so don't cut out lots of old wood when pruning or you won't get much of a crop. One nice problem with redcurrants is that they can fruit so prolifically that the weight of the fruit bends and even breaks branches. If it looks like there is a lot of fruit developing, support the branches by tying to wire or even to a cane.

When the berries develop and turn red they may look ripe but taste a couple before harvesting them. They often take a week or two to develop the sweetness despite looking ready. The same applies to white currants, which are exactly the same as their red relatives except for colour.

The most popular variety of redcurrant is the Jonkheer van Tets Dutch type but for pot growing and tight spaces I would grow Stanza which is compact, heavy cropping and has a lovely deep-coloured berry.

Whichever variety or method you use, don't forget to protect against the birds who will strip them bare before you're out of bed in the morning.

Gooseberries

The days may be past when the gooseberry was called 'The English Fruit' by the French and was far more popular than the tasteless sweetened water pulp they now send us called Golden Delicious, but why not rediscover a superb flavour our great grandparents loved?

Fig. 27. Half Standard gooseberry in a pot.

Even if you have room to grow in the garden, I would suggest growing in a pot as a half-standard. That is a straight stem running a couple of feet up to a bush, similar to decorative bay trees.

The reason is that they have wicked thorns that will go through thick gardening gloves like a hot knife through butter. So pruning is one of those jobs you are tempted to put off and once they're a tangled mass on the ground the temptation is to get rid and grow something less vicious.

As a half-standard though, you can prune easily; rotating the pot instead of trying to stretch over the plant to get to the back. They look good too, especially in a more formal patio setting. You can, of course, grow a standard in a border if you prefer.

They'll grow well in shade and can even thrive trained on a north-facing wall so freeing up space for your sun-loving crops. They like a rich soil, so treat as the currants, providing plenty of nutrients to keep them productive.

The berries take some time to develop on the bush, becoming sweeter as they grow. If you take a picking or two fairly early, ideal for jam, the remaining fruits will swell better and become sweeter, so well suited for eating raw with just a little sugar and cream.

At one time there were dozens of varieties available but as the popularity has dwindled so has the number on the market. Invicta is a good standard, offering a green berry that's a good all-rounder. Whinham's Industry is the one to consider for a red variety.

Goji Berries

I'd better come clean here. No matter how wonderful the health benefits and chock full of antioxidants they may be, I think they taste awful. So before growing, pop into a health food shop and try them. Tastes differ and you might think they're the best thing since sliced bread, eat loads and outlive me.

They're tricky to grow from seed so buy plants from a reputable supplier. They're a member of the solanaceae family, as are tomatoes and potatoes, and illegally imported plants were carrying diseases that could potentially devastate our crops. The reputable suppliers are supplying EU grown plants and these are safe.

They're pretty tough by all accounts; coming from the Himalayas you'd expect them to be hardy. They'll grow on most soils but prefer a rich soil and a sunny position. For container growing use a John Innes No. 3 and some slow release general purpose fertilizer each spring. Ensure they have enough water, especially when fruiting, as they prefer a moist soil.

They take a couple of years to start fruiting and come into full production after four years when they're very productive. The flowers appear in early summer so no worries about frost killing the blossom, with the berries being ready to harvest in late autumn.

They are actually very attractive plants, the flowers are delicate and pretty and the berries look attractive against the foliage, even if I don't like the fruit.

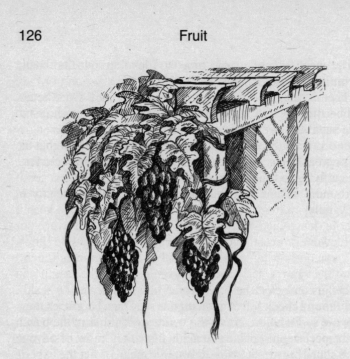

Fig. 28. Grapes on a pergola.

Grapes

You might not think of grapes as a natural candidate for a garden that is tight for space but because they're a climbing plant they're ideal even if you only have a couple of square feet available. I've seen a large pergola covered with a grapevine planted where a single paving slab had been lifted from a patio. The vine even had bunches of grapes hanging down every few feet.

I asked how the vine was pruned and was told that the stems were tied to the beams and any untidy shoots snipped off. So much for the carefully developed theories of pruning the vines and thinning the grapes in the bunches.

You can grow in large containers, but they will actually take up less floor space if you plant into the soil. Initially dig a hole about a foot (30cm) square and half as deep again as the container the vine comes in. If you've got a heavy clay soil, add some gravel to the bottom of the hole to help drain excess water away. Fill with good compost, John Innes No. 3 or a mix of multi-purpose compost and garden soil.

This is just to get the vine off to a good start. Once established the roots will go out and down seeking nutrients and you need not worry about fertilizing, etc. I think the reason my friend's vine did so well, despite being in a patio, was that the roots were down and spread under the hardcore and concrete. The only thing vines hate in the soil is water logging.

Pruning should be undertaken in winter when the leaves have fallen or the vine may bleed and lose strength. To keep it simple, leave the shoots you want to grow up and over your framework or even up a trellis on a wall. Trim any side shoots that you don't want to grow on back to about an inch (2.5cm) from the stem. Once the leading stems are to the length you want, just cut them after a bud.

If you're really into producing the best dessert grapes, then you are supposed to reduce the number of grapes in the bunch with special vine scissors, but I really don't know of anyone who actually does that nowadays. Still, that's what the experts say to do.

There are, as you might imagine with an important commercial crop, many varieties that you can buy of dessert grapes, wine grapes and 'all-rounders'. Your choice will depend on your location to some degree. Most dessert grapes really need a greenhouse to be reliable but if you have a very sheltered spot in the south, then you can try them.

9

HERBS

Herbs are so useful in the kitchen and often so much better fresh that I'm surprised everyone doesn't grow them. They are ideal for the small space grower and especially for the grower who doesn't have much time to spare. Unlike those pampered vegetables, herbs seem to thrive on neglect. Many of our herbs come from sunny Mediterranean hillsides, growing on thin, poor, sandy soils with infrequent rain and being nibbled by passing goats as they're herded between pastures.

So it's no surprise that the ideal growing medium for many of them (see Composts, page 51) is low in nutrients and free draining. Herbs don't like heavy clay soils but they've not had the toughness bred out of them as vegetables have and will often succeed where they're not supposed to anyway. In fact, mint can be as troublesome as any invasive weed if not controlled.

In a small garden they're decorative enough to make a very attractive mixed border, especially if a south-facing sunny border is available, with taller herbs like rosemary to the rear.

One traditional way to grow herbs is in a herb wheel. Usually these are made of bricks set on end in a circle with the spokes of the wheel creating separate compartments. The compartments stop the stronger plants and keep everything in order for you. Larger wheels, around 4 feet (just over 1 metre) in diameter, can have a circular paving slab in the centre with a tub. You're not limited to brick though, you can use upended wine bottles or, less formally, rockery style stones. Because the wheel stands proud of the soil level, in effect it's a raised bed that you can fill with your herb compost mix.

Herbs can form a decorative centre piece in a lawn or even a sidepiece to a driveway. Since your culinary herbs will do perfectly well in pots, a decorative bed covered in gravel, with the pots sunk into the soil, will produce a low maintenance but productive addition to the garden even if you have space to spare.

At the other extreme, if you've no space at all you can still grow a selection of the smaller herbs on a window sill. Everyone has room for a few herbs somewhere.

I've covered the common culinary herbs below but there's no reason why you can't expand into medicinal herbs as well if you want. Don't forget that whatever method you use to grow them, herbs really benefit from a sunny spot.

Drying Herbs

We cook all the year round but our herbs are not always available. Luckily it's easy to dry herbs and keep a store to use through the winter.

Herbs intended for drying should be gathered on a warm dry day, not after rain, and before the sun has warmed the leaves and begun evaporating the essential oils. Pick them just before they come into flower as after flowering the leaves start to toughen up.

Remove any dead or withered leaves, then tie in small bunches by the stems and blanch in boiling water for just a few seconds. Shake off any excess water and leave to dry, or pat dry on a tea towel or kitchen roll.

Wrap your herb bunch loosely in muslin and hang up to dry in a warm place, such as over a cooker or in an airing cupboard. The time to dry will vary according to how warm they are and the amount of draught – from 1 to 4 days is usual. The drying process is complete when the main stems of the herbs crack, rather than bend, and the leaves are brittle.

You can also dry your herbs in a microwave if you've nowhere to air dry them. This is a simple and easy process but you do need to pay careful attention to what you are doing. Lay down two sheets of absorbent kitchen roll and then put a layer of herbs down, then another layer of

Fig. 29. Bunches of herbs drying in the kitchen.

paper towel. Use the microwave on high for 1 minute, then
in bursts of 30 seconds, moving the herbs around and
checking the dryness frequently. The whole process should
take no longer than 3 minutes.

You can also dry in a conventional oven. Place in a cool
oven, at a temperature between 45°C/110°F/Gas Mark 0 and
55°C/130°F/Gas Mark 0. The herbs should be dried until
they are crisp. If the drying process is continuous, this takes
about 1 hour (on a rack above the stove it will take 3–4
hours). If drying sprigs or stalks of herbs in the oven, turn
them over halfway through the drying period to ensure even
drying.

Once dry you can hang in bunches in the kitchen or place
them in a tea towel and run over with a rolling pin. Pick
out the stalks and then store in airtight jars. If stored in
glass bottles, protect them from the light to conserve the
colour.

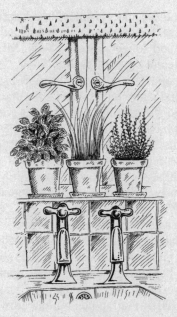

Fig. 30. Herbs in pots on the window sill.

Freezing Herbs

Some herbs such as chives really aren't suitable for drying and basil always loses a lot of flavour when dried but you can still store them for use all year round in cooking by freezing. Pick your herbs as for drying, while at their best, rinse off and remove any stalks, etc.

Put the leaves into a blender and add about a quarter by volume of water and whiz into a paste and then transfer into an ice cube tray. Just pop a cube or two into the dish as you cook.

Basil

You can find basil in small pots in supermarkets nowadays and can keep on a window sill but it don't last long. The suppliers tend to sow too many seeds for the pot in order to develop a bunch quickly but the pot becomes overcrowded in the longer run.

You can split these and transplant into larger pots but it is a little hit and miss. If you grow your own basil from seed you will get better and longer lasting plants. More importantly, you can try different types of basil.

The most popular and well known basil is Basilico Genovese. As the name tells you, it's the Italian type with a strong scent and flavour. For something a little different try Sweet Green, which has a hint of mint in the flavour, or one of the Thai basils, Siam Queen being the best example.

Whichever variety you grow, the method is basically the same. Sow the seeds shallowly and thinly between late February and early May into a small pot indoors at a temperature around 20°C.

Once germinated, which takes a week or two, and the seedlings are large enough to handle, transplant to 3 inch (8cm) pots and grow on to develop a good rootball. If they're to go outside, harden off slowly. Basil does not like cold shocks and a frost will be fatal. Once the main stem reaches about 8 inches (20cm) tall, pinch out the growing tip and this will encourage bushier growth.

Basil is a good companion plant for tomatoes and is said to repel pests. I've read that you can make an organic insecticide from basil, but haven't tried it myself so cannot speak for how effective it may be.

Bay Tree

Visiting a friend whose front door boasted a well shaped bay tree in a pot to either side, I was amazed when she said she was out of bay leaves for a bouquet garni. Yes, those decorative bay trees you buy from the nursery are the same and you can just pick a few leaves as required for your culinary needs.

You may be surprised to find out that if you just planted a bay into the soil and left it to its own devices, eventually it would grow to 40 feet (12 metres) high and 30 feet (9 metres) wide; dominating a large garden never mind a small one. Yet it is ideal for pot growing, but not to that size!

You can start from seed but it is tricky and far easier to buy a small plant from a nursery. Smaller plants are cheaper than larger to buy, so I'll assume that's your starting point.

When you get your plant home, move it into a pot the next size up but do not use the herb compost mix. The bay will do best in John Innes No. 3 loam based compost, but do ensure good drainage in the pot. Either add some slow release fertilizer like Osmacote or liquid feed fortnightly from late spring through the summer with a general purpose fertilizer.

Bay is unusual in that it doesn't mind being root bound in the pot, so when it reaches the final size you want it to be, just stop moving it on each year. A 5 foot (1.5 metre) bay will do perfectly well in a 12 inch (30cm) pot but may look unbalanced and tend to blow over in strong winds. A decorative half barrel or stone tub is ideal.

Thereafter, carefully change the top inch (2.5cm) of compost for fresh each spring and halve the amount of fertilizer given while growing it up. Bays are shallow rooted and I wouldn't try other plants in the same pot as you are likely to damage the roots.

Another reason bays are best grown in pots, in the UK at least, is that they are not very hardy and in really cold weather will need protection or moving to a sheltered spot. Ours moves from the top of the garden to the patio by the house for the winter where the extra shelter affords some protection. If it is going to get below –5°C, wrap with horticultural fleece or bubble wrap.

You can prune your bay each spring to develop the shape you want. A pyramid, Christmas tree style is easy but the standard bay 'ball on a stick' requires a little more effort.

To achieve a ball standard, choose a plant with a straight central stem and remove all the lower side shoots, leaving the top shoots and growing tip until the plant is about 8 inches (20cm) higher than the final required height.

Then cut out the growing tip of the leaders, which will encourage it to bush and just snip with secateurs to produce the globe. The trimmings can be dried and stored in airtight jars for use in the kitchen.

Borage

Borage does not dry well so is best used fresh. The flowers and young leaves make an attractive salad garnish with a mild cucumber flavour. They're also used in gin based cocktails and Pimms, of course.

Borage will grow to about 30 inches (75cm) high and is quite a straggly plant so not ideal for pot growing but will do fine in a herb wheel (see page 128) or patch in the border. If pot growing just use multi-purpose compost rather than the herb mix as borage likes a richer soil than most herbs.

Sow directly from March to May and thin to about 6 inches (15cm) apart, which is overcrowding but allows the plants to support each other.

Chervil

Chervil is better known and more utilized in Europe than Britain yet it is a tasty and versatile herb which goes well with fish and meat. The flavour is a little like a cross between aniseed and caraway. It's also one of the few leaf herbs that can be obtained through the winter if a coldframe or shelter is available. You can also grow in a pot in the window sill to have a winter supply available.

Chervil will also grow in partial shade, making good use of hard to use areas.

Sow directly into ordinary compost or a border from March through the summer, every two or three weeks to provide a continual supply, thinning to 6 inches (15cm) apart.

The leaves are ready for picking after just six to eight weeks. It grows to about 18 inches (45cm) high but is better picked young before it runs to flower.

Chives

Chives are ideal for pot growing and very easy to look after so are ones to put on the 'must grow' list. There are basically two varieties: ordinary chives with an onion flavour and Chinese garlic chives with a mild garlic flavour. The Chinese variety has slightly broader leaves than the onion type. They're a handy herb to have by the kitchen door as they're best used really fresh.

The flowers are edible and what appears to be a globe shape at first look turns out to be made up of many small flowers. The problem is that allowing the flowers to form stops the leaves from growing so, if you want the leaves, remove flower stalks as soon as they form. The flower stalks are inedible.

Start by sowing the seeds thinly in small pots or seed tray modules in a warm place (20–25°C) from March through to July. They can take three weeks to germinate, so patience is required. Thin a little if very crowded but otherwise just transplant into multi-purpose compost in 8 inch (20cm) pots or a 6 inch (15cm) pot for growing in the kitchen widow through the winter.

Snip off leaves at soil level with sharp scissors as required to use. Feed monthly with general purpose fertilizer and water when dry – couldn't be easier.

Chives are perennial so although they die back for the winter, they come back in spring. In the spring, take out of the pot and cut into two plants and re-pot. They are fairly hardy but don't like really cold weather so move to shelter if the thermometer goes below -5°C.

Coriander

Coriander has become a popular herb in Britain as the popularity of Indian foods has grown and many recipes call for the addition of fresh coriander leaves. The seeds of the coriander are also used of course. When buying seed do check the description as some varieties are bred not to bolt (run to seed) more for the leaves, others for the seed and some are dual-purpose.

Relatively new British breeding has come up with 'cut and come again' varieties like Calypso and Confetti, which can be cropped three times before exhausting the plant – great for easy home growing.

Coriander is suitable for pot growing but it does need a deep pot as it has a long tap root. This tap root is the reason that coriander does not take well to being transplanted and should be sown in its final position.

If you are growing for the seeds, choose the sunniest and hottest place you have in the garden; conversely if you do not want the plant to run to seed, choose a spot with partial shade. When growing for leaves, pick off any flowers as soon as seen to prevent running to seed.

For a supply all summer, apart from the cut and come again type, sow sequentially every three weeks or so between March and September, protecting with cloches, etc in cold weather. If the leaves start to yellow or growth seems poor, feed with a general liquid fertilizer.

Dill

Dill is a decorative plant with fern like foliage and a delicate aniseed like flavour that will do well in pots. It does take a bit of room, growing to 36 inches (90cm) high and an 8–12 inch (20–30cm) pot is best with some space around.

Sow into 3 inch (8cm) pots in early spring, moving on to a larger final pot when about 6 inches (15cm) tall, sheltering with fleece or cloches if the weather turns cold. Successionally sow at monthly intervals after if you want a continual supply.

Dill prefers full sun but will thrive in light shade. The plants have a tendency to flop over so put some small canes in the pot and tie in to support them.

Dill will dry or freeze to store for the kitchen but add into dishes at the end of the cooking as the delicate flavour is easily lost.

Fennel

Fennel has a similar flavour to dill but needs a lot more room and is grown more as a vegetable for the bulb. I'd suggest it's not one for container growing but have been told that it can be grown in 8 inch (20cm) pots, one plant per pot with plenty of space around for the foliage.

Avoid growing next to dill as they can cross, spoiling the flavour of both.

Lemon Grass

Lemon grass is a basic ingredient in much of south east Asian cuisine. For those wanting to make their own Thai curries and Vietnamese fish dishes living outside of the cities it can be hard to obtain. Luckily you can grow your own but it isn't too easy.

Start off by sowing indoors in February, keeping the temperature around 20–25°C. A plastic bag around the pot will help in keeping the humidity high which is needed for germination and early growth. Lemon grass takes about three weeks to germinate; don't give up too soon!

When the seedlings are large enough to handle, move to 3 inch (8cm) pots and for outdoor planting begin hardening off slowly. As you may imagine, our conditions in Britain are somewhat colder than it really likes. If you have a greenhouse or conservatory it will do better than outside.

Finally pot up into 10–12 inch (25–30cm) pots. It is a perennial but to get it through the winter you have to keep it where the minimum temperature will not fall below 7°C.

Marjoram and Oregano

Once again, just like broccoli and calabrese, our imprecise naming of culinary plants causes confusions. The same plant may well be described as oregano in one nursery and marjoram in another. Even the experts disagree!

To try and simplify, all marjoram varieties are oreganos but the marjorams available in the UK tend to be more tender and treated as annuals while the types described as oregano have a stronger flavour and are treated as perennials.

The good news is that, whatever they're called, they are suitable for pot growing.

Oregano is easiest to grow from plants bought from the nursery, a compact variety being best for pots and small herb gardens. Use the general herb compost mix in a 12 inch (30cm) pot and ensure drainage is good. It won't tolerate being waterlogged. It's another herb that thrives on neglect so only feed sparingly if the plant is looking yellow and poorly.

The leaves should be harvested before the flowers form in July as the flavour becomes somewhat bitter after this. You can trim off the flowers to extend the harvest time but oregano will dry well and we prefer to use it as a dried herb rather than fresh.

After three years the plants will be getting very straggly and woody, so replace with fresh stock. Although reasonably hardy, bring the pots into some shelter in very cold weather or cover with fleece, etc.

The marjorams are, as I said, best treated as annuals and grown from seed. They'll work as a window sill plant as well. Sow shallowly from late winter to early summer in a small pot, covered with a plastic bag to hold moisture, on the window sill. Germination can take three weeks. Once large enough to handle, move on into 3 inch (8cm) pots of ordinary multi-purpose compost and from there to their final home in either a large 12 inch (30cm) pot filled with the herb mix compost or into a border.

Unlike oregano, marjoram is best used as a fresh herb and goes well in any tomato/pasta dish.

Mint

Mint is one herb I would always grow in a pot, or at least a bottomless pot sunk into the ground, because if you do not constrain it, it will spread like a weed smothering neighbouring plants in its quest to take over the garden.

If you thought mint was just mint, think again. There are hundreds of varieties including apple mint, spearmint, pineapple mint, orange mint, liquorice, peppermint and even chocolate mint. The difference in flavour is remarkable and it can be fun to add some different flavours to a salad and watch visitors' faces as they try to work out what exactly they are eating.

Although you can start from seed, with the unusual flavours there is a wider choice available as plants. The National Herb Centre near Banbury (see Contacts) stock around two dozen types of mint.

If growing in a border, take a large pot (the ex-flower

buckets are ideal) and cut out the base, sinking the pot into the ground with about an inch (2.5cm) protruding. Transplant into ordinary multi-purpose compost mixed 50/50 with John Innes.

Pick the leaves as you need; giving the plant a good haircut in summer will encourage bushy growth. Give a general purpose liquid feed monthly or at least if the plant looks sickly.

Mint will fill its container and become pot bound in a season so in the early spring, as growth starts back, remove from the container and cut the root ball in half or even quarters and re-pot.

Mint will dry well or freeze to store for use through the winter. Alternatively, you can make a mint sauce base that will last for six months. Take ½ pint (285ml) of malt vinegar and dissolve 6 oz (170g) of sugar in it over heat and boil for 1 minute. Then add 4 oz (100g) of washed and chopped mint leaves and stir well. Allow to cool and pot into clean jars and seal. When you want some mint sauce, just thin some of your base with vinegar to the desired consistency and serve.

Parsley

There are two main types of parsley: flat leaved and curly leaved. It is said that the curly leaved varieties were developed due to an unfortunate resemblance between flat leaved parsley and the common weed fool's parsley or dog parsley that is slightly poisonous being related to the hemlock family.

Although we generally eat parsley as a garnish or use it as a flavouring herb rather than a vegetable, it's actually nutritious and vitamin rich. Parsley has a flavour reminiscent of celery (they're both in the same crop family of Umbellifera) and they combine to make a lovely soup. You can also briefly deep fry parsley and serve as a separate vegetable.

Parsley is perfect for pot growing and will thrive as a window sill herb year round. Parsley is slow to germinate and even for outdoor planting is best started indoors in small pots or modules, moving on to 4 inch (10cm) pots, one plant per pot, as they grow. Avoid over wetting the compost as the seeds are prone to rot off.

Of the curled leaf varieties, Favorit and Moss Curled both have the RHS Award of Garden Merit and are easy to cultivate.

The flat leaved varieties, often called French or Italian, tend to have a stronger flavour.

Rosemary

To us, lamb without rosemary just isn't lamb and on those rare days in the summer when the barbecue sees action, some rosemary on the coals fills the patio with that gorgeous aroma.

Rosemary is more of a shrub than herb but it will do well in a pot as well as the border. Like the bay, rosemary is best bought as a plant rather than seed and cultivation is similar; except rosemary doesn't appreciate being pot bound as the bay does.

Try to avoid disturbing the roots when potting on or transplanting and ensure good drainage. If planting into a border and the soil is heavy, dig the hole about a foot to 18 inches (30–45cm) deep and put some gravel and sand in to ensure the roots don't get waterlogged in the winter.

It also seems to appreciate a tablespoon of lime dusted around the plant in the winter as it doesn't like an acid soil. Feed monthly in pots through the spring and summer with a general purpose liquid feed or use a slow release fertilizer in spring like Osmacote.

Rosemary isn't as amenable to topiary as the bay is but a clip in spring and autumn will keep it tidy. Many varieties have a trailing habit so can look a little untidy to say the least. For pot growing, I'd recommend an upright variety, my favourite being the quaintly named Miss Jessops Upright. Miss Jessops is fairly easy to obtain, looks well and has very aromatic foliage but there are around 20 other varieties available in the UK. Some are better than others for culinary use and some better just used as a decorative shrub.

Prostrate rosemary is very low growing, almost a ground cover plant, ideal for pot growing. Its trailing habit means it overhangs and softens the edge of the pot. It's also good in a large wall mounted pot or window box for the same reason.

If your shrub starts to get too big for your situation, then you can easily replace it for free by taking a cutting in May or early June. Snip off a 3 inch (8cm) cutting from the end of a young shoot and strip the leaves from the lower half.

Dip the root end into hormonal rooting powder and then stick into a 3 inch (8cm) pot of multi-purpose compost. Cover the pot with a plastic bag to keep the moisture in and keep in a warm place but out of direct sunlight. In six to eight weeks it should have rooted and you will have a new plant.

Sage

Sage has been used since at least Roman times as a medicinal herb and even today trials have been carried out to test those medicinal properties. Sage was reported to have some effect in boosting memory and in the management of Alzheimer's disease. However, we just like it in sage and onion stuffing. Sage dries well and can be frozen to provide year round supplies.

It's ideal for pot growing and will do well indoors on a sunny window sill. It can be started from seed but is far easier to grow on from a nursery bought plant. Sage prefers to be on the dry side so make sure there's good drainage in the pot and occasionally miss out in the watering.

Sage can be a bit of a straggler and wind can cause the woody stems to break so tying to a short stake is a good idea. Feed sparingly, otherwise it is one of those plants that thrives on neglect.

There are a number of varieties of sage available – purple sage having, as the name suggests, purple leaves. There are variegated leaf types and intriguingly pineapple and black-currant sages which have more of the scent than flavour of those fruits.

Common sage is hardy but the unusual varieties are frequently tender and need to be sheltered from frost.

Sage tends to lose its strength after three or four years but is easy enough to propagate from a cutting taken in the spring – just follow the same method as for rosemary.

Tarragon

Tarragon is an essential herb for French cuisine with its vanilla and aniseed flavour. There are two types – French and Russian tarragon – with the French generally agreed to have a finer flavour. Tarragon is always a component in Béarnaise sauce and tarragon vinegar works well as a salad dressing.

It's best started from plants rather than seed and the French type can only be started from plants as the seed always reverts to Russian. It's a vigorous plant, growing to 4 feet (120cm) tall but can be grown in large pots so long as you replace it after three years when it will be root bound and strangling itself.

It's easy to propagate from cuttings though, so you only ever need to buy one plant. On the third year start a replacement, ready to replace your pot-bound plant. You can remove the pot-bound plant and divide and re-pot but I've not found this too successful.

Thyme

Thyme is one of those herbs that seems to have been left behind a little in our celebrity chef culture's search for the new and exotic. Despite that, it's still versatile and enhances everything from stuffings, soups and stews to omelettes and scrambled eggs.

It's actually a relative of the mints but has an unmistakeably different flavour.

Thyme is fine for pot growing and a window sill pot will keep you going when the outdoors plants are dormant in winter. Thyme will dry well and can be frozen for use in winter if you prefer.

You can start from seeds but they are easier to start from nursery bought plants. The nurseries can offer a wider selection than those easily available from the seed merchants although personally I would stay with common thyme.

With seeds, sow any time from late winter to early summer in a small pot in a polythene bag, to retain the moisture, at a temperature above 18°C. When large enough to handle, transplant into 3 inch (8cm) pots of herb mix and from there into 8 inch (20cm) or larger pots. Feed monthly with general purpose liquid feed during the growing season.

After three years the plants start to get quite woody so remove from the pot and divide the roots to form new plants.

GLOSSARY

Some of the more common gardening terms you might come across.

Allium
The Latin name of the onion family which includes onion, shallot, garlic, chives and leek.

Blanch
To deprive a plant of light to produce a tender growth as with chicory, celery and leeks.

Blight
A fungal disease, usually of potatoes and tomatoes.

Bolt
When a plant prematurely produces flowers or seeds at the expense of the edible crop. Most often affects onions and lettuce.

Bordeaux Mixture
A mixture of copper sulphate and slaked lime used to control blight in potatoes and tomatoes.

Brassica
General term for members of the cabbage family from the Latin *Brassicaceae*.

Chitting
(of potatoes)

Allowing the seed potatoes to form shoots prior to planting.

Chitting
(of seeds)

Germinating seeds before sowing. Also useful for establishing viability and germination rate of seeds, see page 54.

Cloche

Any kind of (transparent) low-lying temporary shelter for use on open ground.

Club-root

Serious soil-borne fungal disease affecting all brassicas.

Coldframe

A low, glass-covered structure to provide sheltered growing conditions.

Companion
Planting

Planting two different species next to each other to benefit the growth of both. Usually to deter pests by disguising one partner or repelling pests from one plant by use of the other.

Compost

Term used for a growing medium produced by the decomposition of organic matter. Also commercial composts which include other materials such as peat or fibre, minerals and fertilizers, etc.

Crop Rotation

Moving crops around to avoid the build-up of pests and disease and to best utilize available nutrients.

Cucubit

The plant family that includes cucumbers, marrows, squashes, pumpkins and courgettes.

Cultivar

A variety or type of plant; for example,

Sungold and Gardener's Delight are cultivars of tomatoes.

Damping Down   Raising the humidity in a greenhouse by watering the floors and/or staging. Tends to lower the temperature and reduce water loss from plants.

Damping Off   Death of seedlings due to overly wet, crowded or poorly ventilated conditions.

Double Digging   A method of deeply digging over land, incorporating organic matter to increase the depth of topsoil, improve drainage and fertility.

Earthing Up   Process of drawing up loose earth around the stems or even over the foliage (especially potatoes) of plants to improve the crop and/or protect against frost.

Eelworm   Tiny transparent worm which adversely affects yields and/or quality of several plant varieties, notably potato and onion.

Flea Beetle   Insect pest that mainly damages radish, swedes, turnip and Chinese cabbage.

Fleece   Horticultural fleece is a lightweight, translucent cloth that allows water to pass through and is used to provide shelter to plants and protection from pests.

Forcing   Process of making a plant grow in the dark to produce a tender leaf or fruit as with rhubarb.

Germinate   Not all seeds are viable, those that
                         develop are said to germinate. Also the
                         process of growing a seedling from a
                         seed.

Germination Rate   The number of viable seeds that develop
                         against the total number of seeds.

Gone Over   Term used when a crop has gone past its
                         optimum harvest point.

Green Manure   A crop grown to retain and provide
                         nutrients and organic matter in the soil to
                         improve fertility.

Hardy   A plant which is tolerant of frosts/winter
                         conditions in the area in which it is being
                         grown.

Haulm   The stems and foliage of a plant, usually
                         used in regard to potatoes.

Heel In   Method of holding a plant in the soil for
                         later use.

Heritage Variety   Old variety of plant, usually harder to
                         obtain than modern varieties but often
                         with fine flavour.

Inter-planting   Planting two or more species to
                         maximize use of space such as a fast-
                         growing plant between slow-growing
                         plants.

Legume   The bean family of plants noted for the
                         ability to fix nitrogen from the air.

Module   Section or cell of an insert put into a seed
                         tray to divide it up into separate pots.

Mulch To place a layer of material on the surface of the soil. Usually to provide nutrients or prevent water loss or inhibit weed growth.

Offset A short lateral shoot by which certain plants are propagated.

Pinch Out The action of removing the growing tip of a shoot, to produce a more bushy plant, also known as stopping. Also the removal of small side shoots by using the end of the finger and thumb to pinch the stem until it is separated from the main stem.

Pot On, Pot Along The action of placing a seedling into a pot and of moving a plant from one pot to a larger pot as it grows.

Riddle Basically a coarse sieve made of plastic or metal to sift compost and soil.

Rust Describes different fungal diseases by the appearance of orange patches that look like rust. Often affects alliums, especially leeks and comfrey.

Seed Potato Small potato used to start the new crop.

Set Usually as in 'onion set', a small immature bulb which has been raised from seed before having development stopped by the grower. The resulting bulb is then set the following spring so as to complete its growth in one season.

Spacing The distance required between plants to

maximize the crop and efficiently use the space.

Station Sowing   Sowing of seeds in their final position. Usually two or more seeds are sown and then only the strongest seedling is allowed to grow on.

Stop or Stopping   See Pinch Out.

Successional Sowing   Method of sowing crops at intervals, usually every fortnight or three weeks, to provide crops ready to harvest over a period rather than in one go.

Tender   Describes a plant which is not tolerant of frosts or even cold weather in the area in which it is being grown. Typically requiring a greenhouse or coldframe.

Thinning, Thin Out   Removal of seedlings or small plants to permit others space to develop to their full potential. Because seeds may not all germinate, we sow more than required then thin out to the required spacing.

Transplant   To re-plant, usually, into final cropping position.

Truss   Used mostly with tomatoes to refer to the cluster of fruits on a stem. Vine tomatoes in a shop are more properly called a truss of tomatoes.

Tuber   The thickened portion of a root such as the actual potato in a potato plant.

Underplanting   Planting a low growing plant under a tall growing plant, such as strawberries around the base of an apple tree, thereby maximizing use of space.

Volunteer

A plant growing in the wrong place after self-seeding or re-growth of a missed tuber when lifting (main culprits are potatoes and Jerusalem artichokes).

White Rot

A serious disease of onion, shallot, leek, garlic and chives. It is soil-borne, very persistent, and can lie dormant for up to fifteen years.

Wireworm

Small worm pest mainly of potatoes, particularly troublesome when the ground is recently converted from grass-land.

FURTHER INFORMATION AND CONTACTS

My Website – Allotment Vegetable Growing
www.allotment.org.uk

On my own website I've got quite a few articles that I hope you will find helpful and interesting in addition to this book. Also for specific advice and answers to questions we have a popular forum with over 10,000 members. There's rarely a question someone can't answer for you.

Organizations

Garden Organic has been promoting organic growing for 50 years. When it started it was very much a voice in the wilderness but now it's very much mainstream. It runs a number of demonstration gardens and offers advice to members.

Garden Organic
(formerly the Henry Doubleday Research Organization)
Garden Organic Ryton
Coventry
Warwickshire
CV8 3LG
www.gardenorganic.org.uk

The National Vegetable Society is, as the name says, firmly

aimed at the vegetable grower. It organizes shows, trains and examines judges and provides lecturers. It has a network of local societies which meet to discuss and share information on vegetables. Since most of the top show growers grow in containers and are members, it's a very useful source of help for the small space grower. I'm a member and serve on the National Executive at the time of writing.

The National Vegetable Society
c/o National Secretary
Mr D S Thornton FNVS
36 The Ridings
Ockbrook
Derby
DE72 3SF
www.nvsuk.org.uk

The RHS has to be the premier gardening society in the world. Its website is a wonderful resource.

The Royal Horticultural Society
80 Vincent Square
London
SW1P 2PE
www.rhs.org.uk

Mail Order Garden Equipment Suppliers
There are many suppliers of gardening equipment but these are companies I personally know offer a good range at reasonable prices and a good quality of service.

Two Wests & Elliott Ltd
Unit 4 Carrwood Road
Sheepbridge Industrial Estate
Chesterfield
Derbyshire S41 9RH
www.twowests.co.uk

Harrod Horticultural
Pinbush Road
Lowestoft
Suffolk NR33 7NL
www.harrodhorticultural.com

Some UK Seed Suppliers

Thompson & Morgan
Poplar Lane
Ipswich
Suffolk
IP8 3BU
www.thompson-morgan.com

Suttons Seeds
Woodview Road
Paignton
Devon
TQ4 7NG
www.suttons.co.uk

Dobies Seeds
Long Road
Paignton
Devon
TQ4 7SX
www.dobies.co.uk

Specialist Vegetable Seed Suppliers

Medwyns of Anglesey
Llanor
Ffordd Hen Ysgol
Llanfairpwllgwyngyll
Anglesey
LL61 5RZ
www.medwynsofanglesey.co.uk

Select Seeds
58 Bentinck Road
Shuttlewood
Chesterfield
S44 6RQ
www.selectseeds.co.uk

Herbs

While the general seed suppliers can supply herbs and fruit bushes, for herbs I would suggest a visit to The National Herb Centre at Warmington, near Banbury in Oxfordshire. It has a huge range and will happily give sound advice. It also supplies by mail order.

The National Herb Centre
Banbury Road
Warmington
OX17 1DF
www.herbcentre.co.uk

Fruit

I've found Ken Muir's nursery to be very helpful. It supplies a good range including minarettes and the duo-minarettes, family trees, etc. Its expertise has been proven by having won 12 RHS Gold Medals.

Ken Muir Ltd
Honeypot Farm
Rectory Road
Weeley Heath
Clacton-on-Sea
Essex
CO16 9BJ
www.kenmuir.co.uk

There are, obviously, many other nurseries supplying fruit trees and I'd suggest only using suppliers who are willing to provide advice and suggest varieties for your specific locality. Many good local nurseries will order in for you as well and surprisingly can be cheaper than going directly to their suppliers. Fruit trees and bushes are quite an expensive long-term investment and it can be years before you realize that a mistake has been made with your purchase.

INDEX

Also by John Harrison

VEGETABLE GROWING MONTH BY MONTH

The down-to-earth guide that takes you through the vegetable year

John shows you when you should sow your seeds, dig your plot and harvest your crops.

'Harrison's book is crammed with useful information, unencumbered by any trendy graphics… it's perfect for all those gardeners who just want a book to tell them exactly what to do, and when.'
Emma Townshend in the *Independent on Sunday*

THE ESSENTIAL ALLOTMENT GUIDE

How to get the best out of your plot

John shows how to clear an allotment and safely dispose of rubbish, plan your plot for maximum production and keep the children occupied and helping.

LOW-COST LIVING

Live better, spend less

John's simple, tried and tested methods will help you to enjoy a better standard of living while saving money and helping the environment.

EASY JAMS, CHUTNEYS AND PRESERVES

Val and John Harrison show how to make your own jams, jellies, marmalades, chutneys, pickles, fruit butters and fruit cheeses.